Words: The Foundation of Literacy

Words

THE FOUNDATION OF LITERACY

Dale D. Johnson

Bonnie Johnson

WESTVIEW
PRESS

A Member of the Perseus Books Group

Published by Westview Press,
A Member of the Perseus Books Group

Find us on the World Wide Web at www.westviewpress.com.

Every effort has been made to secure required permissions to use all images, maps,
and other art included in this volume.

Westview Press books are available at special discounts for bulk purchases in
the United States by corporations, institutions, and other organizations.
For more information, please contact the Special Markets Department at the
Perseus Books Group, 2300 Chestnut Street, Suite 200, Philadelphia, PA 19103, or
call (800) 810-4145, ext. 5000, or e-mail special.markets@perseusbooks.com.

Designed by Brent Wilcox

Library of Congress Cataloging-in-Publication Data
Johnson, Dale D.
    Words : the foundation of literacy / Dale D. Johnson, Bonnie Johnson.
        p.   cm.
    Includes bibliographical references and index.
    ISBN 978-0-8133-4415-7 (alk. paper)
    1. Vocabulary—Study and teaching.   2. Language arts—Correlation with
content subjects.   I. Johnson, Bonnie.   II. Title.
    LB1574.5.J65 2011
    372.44—dc22

                                                                        2010006309

10 9 8 7 6 5 4 3 2 1

To Stanley and Mary Anna Von Hoff
for watching over Green Acres

Contents

Foreword

Vocabulary knowledge is essential to learning to read. As early as 1925, reading-comprehension expert Guy Whipple argued that widening and enriching one's reading vocabulary are essential to reading comprehension. Some years later, Frederick B. Davis identified two skills in reading comprehension: word knowledge (i.e., vocabulary) and reasoning. The importance of vocabulary for reading continues to be viewed as important. In *Preventing Reading Difficulties in Young Children*, for example, Catherine E. Snow, M. Susan Burns, and Peg Griffin identify vocabulary as part of comprehension and, thus, as part of the three groups of skills and abilities that are crucial for early experience in learning to read.[1]

In 2000, the National Reading Panel analyzed instructional research and found that explicit teaching of vocabulary was effective; however, at the time that the Panel issued its report, little or no attention was being paid to explicit vocabulary instruction in some schools.[2] The finding that it was effective eventually found its way into educational policy. More recently, the Institute for Education Sciences published a practice guide recommending explicit vocabulary instruction as a strongly supported practice for adolescents.[3]

Vocabulary appears to be vital to learning to read at all levels. It is especially important for children learning to read. The reason for this concerns a particular combination of factors, including the alphabetic nature of the English language.

Most beginning reading instruction uses some form of decoding of words to speech, based on the alphabetic principle that letters and sounds have a stable relationship to each other. Oral reading becomes the vehicle for learning to read even though highly accomplished (usually older) readers do not overtly translate words into speech. Rather, the ultimate goal of reading is to read silently. The reason for the use of decoding is to capitalize on students' knowledge of oral language.

A common assumption among educators is that most beginning readers have a sizable oral-language vocabulary and a relatively small reading vocabulary. That is, they are believed to know many more words in oral language than words they can recognize in print. Moreover, if the text to be read contains words the children already have in their oral vocabulary, decoding the print to speech will leverage their oral vocabulary to assist in reading comprehension. Of course, the larger the oral vocabulary, the greater the leverage for reading will be.

As it turns out, however, there are great disparities in the size of vocabulary among different groups of students. Betty Hart and Todd R. Risley found that 4-year-olds from professional families had exposure to 42 million words compared with only 13 million words among their counterparts in families who live in poverty.[4] Such disparities last well into the school years, making vocabulary size a powerful variable in school readiness. Nowhere is this correlation more apparent than for English-language learners (ELLs). As noted by Deborah J. Short and Shannon Fitzsimmons, ELLs may have double the work in that they must simultaneously make up for missing early-language instruction and keep up with current acquisition needs.[5] National Literacy Panel findings suggest the importance of oral-language development for literacy.[6] Because vocabulary is an essential part of oral language, it is clear that ELLs are at risk for nonliteracy unless they receive appropriate vocabulary instruction.

Regarding older ELLs, Short and Fitzsimmons make the point that vocabulary acquisition is a particularly critical need. They write:

> The academic vocabulary challenge alone is overwhelming. Consider that high school students are expected to have a vocabulary of approximately 50,000 words to be able to master the increasingly com-

plex coursework of high school and the average student learns 3,000 new words each year. In 4 years, then, the average beginning ELL might learn 12,000 to 15,000 words without targeted interventions, falling far short of the 50,000-word goal. When they have to perform double the work, learning academic English while learning content of multiple subjects, they are at a decided disadvantage in the country's schools.[7]

Despite the importance of *learning* vocabulary, teachers have a hard time *teaching* vocabulary. For many of them, teaching English-language learners is especially difficult—in part, because the languages that ELLs speak are usually closely related to English. In the United States, the majority of students who speak a native language other than English speak Spanish. English-vocabulary learning is easier for Spanish speakers, given that 30–50 percent of educated vocabulary is cognate between the two languages. Among Spanish speakers, the learning of the other 50–70 percent must be provided for. Another challenge is attending to the need for native speakers of noncognate languages to learn English vocabulary. But thus far we have had very little guidance on teaching vocabulary.

In short, learning vocabulary is essential for *all* students. Although Dale and Bonnie Johnson did not set out to focus their book primarily on education, the temptation to think about *Words: The Foundation of Literacy* in that context is irresistible. The book is a valuable and engaging resource that lays out a thorough background of derivations and other information about words and word usages. A particularly useful feature is the strong emphasis on figurative language and words. Idioms and figurative language in general are the most difficult linguistic forms to acquire. Moreover, the book offers a variety of instructional activities, although that is not its sole aim. This is an entertaining work filled with many facts and explanations about words, their origins, and the ways that people perceive, acquire, and access them. *Words: The Foundation of Literacy* is a book that one can read for multiple purposes: curiosity, enjoyment, and pedagogy. It blends linguistics, discourse analysis, education practice, history, and fun.

Most important is that Dale and Bonnie Johnson have written a work that will make vocabulary instruction more effective by bringing it to life for teachers and students.

Michael L. Kamil
Professor, Language Learning and Policy
Stanford University
Stanford, CA

Notes

1. Guy Whipple, ed., *The Twenty-Fourth Yearbook of the National Society for the Study of Education: Report of the National Committee on Reading* (Bloomington, IL: Public School Publishing Company, 1925); Frederick B. Davis, "Two New Measures of Reading Ability," *Journal of Educational Psychology* 33 (1942): 365–372; Catherine E. Snow, M. Susan Burns, and Peg Griffin, eds. (Committee on the Prevention of Reading Difficulties in Young Children), *Preventing Reading Difficulties in Young Children* (Washington, DC: National Academy Press, 1998).

2. National Institute of Child Health and Human Development, *Report of the National Reading Panel. Teaching Children to Read: An Evidence-Based Assessment of the Scientific Research Literature on Reading and Its Implications for Reading Instruction: Reports of the Subgroups* (NIH Publication No. 00–4769) (Washington, DC: U.S. Government Printing Office, 2000).

3. Michael L. Kamil, G. D. Borman, J. Dole, C. C. Kral, T. Salinger, and J. Torgesen, *Improving Adolescent Literacy: Effective Classroom and Intervention Practices: A Practice Guide* (NCEE #2008–4027) (Washington, DC: National Center for Education Evaluation and Regional Assistance, Institute of Education Sciences, U.S. Department of Education, 2008), http://ies.ed.gov/ncee/wwc.

4. Betty Hart and Todd R. Risley, *Meaningful Differences in the Everyday Experience of Young American Children* (Baltimore: P. H. Brookes, 1995).

5. Deborah J. Short and Shannon Fitzsimmons, *Double the Work: Challenges and Solutions to Acquiring Language and Academic Literacy for Adolescent English Language Learners—A Report to Carnegie Corporation of New York* (Washington, DC: Alliance for Excellent Education, 2007).

6. Diane August and Timothy Shanahan, eds., *Developing Literacy in Second-Language Learners: Report of the National Literacy Panel on Language-Minority Children and Youth* (Mahwah, NJ: Lawrence Erlbaum, 2006).

7. Short and Fitzsimmons, *Double the Work*, pp. 26–27. Regarding the "vocabulary of approximately 50,000 words" that high school students are expected to have, see Michael F. Graves, *The Vocabulary Book: Learning and Instruction* (New York: Teachers College Press, 2006), as well as William E. Nagy and Richard C. Anderson, "How Many Words Are There in Printed School English?" *Reading Research Quarterly* 19 (1984): 304–330.

Preface

Each year, my wife and I write a column about literacy entitled "What's Hot, What's Not." The column appears early in the calendar year in *Reading Today*, the widely circulated periodical of the International Reading Association. To assemble our list of hot and not-so-hot topics, we interview twenty-five literacy leaders asking them if a given topic is "hot" (i.e., receiving positive attention) or "not hot." Surprisingly, our column has received a great deal of attention itself. Longer discussions of the results have appeared in a variety of venues. It has been translated into Spanish, replicated in several European countries, and cited in countless educational texts and journal articles. Since that column's inception in 1997, the topic *word meaning/vocabulary* has been on the list. For most of that time, the topic was decidedly cold, whereas other topics such as *phonemic awareness* and *phonics* were perceived to be "very hot." Luckily for children and youth around the country, that situation began to change in 2005, when *word meaning/vocabulary* began to heat up. Since 2005, *word meaning/vocabulary* has been firmly ensconced on a hot, and sometimes very hot, burner. In our column, my wife and I are always careful to warn that "hot" is not synonymous with "important." However, in the case of *word meaning/vocabulary*, most of our literacy leaders would agree that this topic is both hot and important.

Predictably, when a topic becomes hot, numerous books of activities and pedagogical strategies begin to appear on the market. That is certainly true of the topic *word meaning/vocabulary*. A quick perusal of any educational catalog will reveal many recent books on the topic. However,

Words: The Foundation of Literacy is unlike any of those other tomes. Here we do not see endless activity pages or detailed descriptions of methodologies. What Dale and Bonnie Johnson have written is a wonderfully readable volume about our language—about words, the true foundation of language and literacy. Clearly, they both love words and language in all its vagaries. They are what Richard C. Anderson and William E. Nagy would call *lexiphiles*—people who collect words, who relish language and are fascinated by its beauty and complexity.[1] Ah, but you say that you've never heard of a *lexiphile*. Not surprising! It isn't a real word—but it should be and the Johnsons would be prime exemplars of such a term. Their love of language is evident in their writing, and what they choose to write about—idioms, eponyms, toponyms, onomastics, word origins, euphemisms, hyperbole, chiasmus—are all here. And you cannot help but be fascinated by their descriptions.

I have heard the poet Maya Angelou speak of a teacher who inspired her love of language. The teacher was not a particularly nurturing individual, but she was passionate about language and conveyed that passion to the young Maya Angelou. The Johnsons have that same passion for language—for words—and they convey that passion to their readers, including the teachers among them. Those teachers, in turn, will likely instill the same passion for words and language in their students.

I first started teaching at the university level more than thirty years ago. One of the books that inspired me in those first years was a book co-authored by Dale Johnson, *Teaching Reading Vocabulary* (1978).[2] I immediately ordered it as required reading for one of my classes. Since that seminal work, there have been many volumes written on vocabulary instruction, including some by the Johnsons themselves. *Words: The Foundation of Literacy*, however, undoubtedly will join that 1978 work as one of the premier resources for teachers at all levels. After reading it, you too will become a *lexiphile*.

Jack Cassidy
Texas A&M University
Corpus Christi, Texas

Notes

1. Richard C. Anderson and William E. Nagy, "The Vocabulary Conundrum," *American Educator* (Winter 1992): 14–18, 44–47.

2. Dale D. Johnson and P. David Pearson, *Teaching Reading Vocabulary* (New York: Holt, Rinehart and Winston, 1978 [reprinted in 1984]).

Introduction

Words and the meanings of words are not matters merely for the academic amusement of linguists and logisticians, or for the aesthetic delight of poets; they are matters of the profoundest ethical significance to every human being.

—Aldous Huxley, *Words and Their Meanings* (1940)

This is a book about the absorbing world of words. Words are the foundation of literacy, for without words there is no language. Without words there could be no sound structure, no syntax, no grammatical rules. *Words* can be simply defined as linguistic units of sound and print that represent meanings. But as we will show in this book, words are much more complex than that. Some words have multiple meanings, and some meanings are represented by different words. Some words serve more than one grammatical function. Some words have meaning in and of themselves, but other words derive meaning only from their relationship to the words around them.

In his acclaimed work, *The Science of Words*, George A. Miller articulates the essentiality of words to human knowledge:

An inescapable fact that will surely impress anyone who carefully considers the operations of the human mind is how much people know. . . . And one thing that everybody knows is a language, which is itself a very large chunk of knowledge. The major part of that large chunk of knowledge consists of knowing the words of the language. It is not the speech sounds or the rules for generating grammatical sentences that require the most extensive learning. It is the vocabulary: thousands of words, each with its own sound, its own spelling, its own meaning, its own role, its own use, its own history.[1]

And linguist Eve V. Clark's scholarly research compilation on language development begins with these words:

> Words make a language. They are used to talk about everything from beekeeping to bicycling, from navigation to international banking. They supply us with the means for everyday talk about our surroundings and activities, about people, objects, and places, about relations, properties, and states of being. We need them to communicate about events and ideas, technology, science, philosophy, and art.[2]

There is no uncertainty in the minds of these scholars about the indispensability of words to all human endeavors. Psychologist Gerry Altmann frames the fundamental importance of words with this pithy observation: "The advent of the written word must surely rank, together with fire and the wheel, as one of mankind's greatest achievements."[3]

Human language exists to convey, expand, and comprehend meaning. To accomplish this, languages have systems, including the *phonological* (i.e., sounds), *orthographical* (i.e., written symbols), *morphological* (i.e., words and word parts), *syntactic* (i.e., sentences), and *semantic* (i.e., meanings) systems.

The phonological system is composed of *phonemes*, the smallest distinctive speech sounds used in a language. There are approximately forty-four phonemes used in English, depending on a person's dialect. Everything that we say or hear in language uses these forty-four distinct sounds combined in different ways to represent different words.

Related to the phonological system is the written system of a language, called the orthography. In English, the twenty-six letters of the alphabet as well as punctuation marks, numerals, spacing, and logograms (e.g., $, &, %) are used to represent oral language.

The morphological system involves the structure of words and how they are formed. The smallest distinctive units of meaning in a language are called *morphemes*, and there are two types. *Free morphemes* need not be attached to other morphemes. Words are considered free morphemes. *Bound morphemes* also carry meaning, but they cannot stand alone. To the free morpheme *joy* we can add bound morphemes to form *joyful, joyless, enjoyment,* and more.

The syntactic system comprises the rules of language that determine permissible word order and function. It is syntax that enables us to generate sentences and to understand what people say. The sentence *The cat ran up the hill* makes sense, but *Hill cat up the ran the* makes no sense, because it does not follow syntactic rules.

Semantics refers to the meaning system of the language. It consists of the vocabulary of a language, also called its *lexicon*. Semantics additionally refers to other meaningful elements such as idioms (e.g., *in a pickle*), proverbs (e.g., *waste not, want not*), slang (e.g., a *greasy spoon*), and longer units of discourse.

Words: The Foundation of Literacy is a book primarily about words. In this volume, we share our fascination with words as well as the understandings we have gained through decades of lexical research and scholarship. It is through words, we believe, that the wit and wisdom of humankind are enjoyed and understood. We show the versatility of words but also their precision. Sometimes serious and sometimes lighthearted, our goal is that you and your students derive pleasure from words and word study, and that you discover how intriguing words are and how much fun the study of them can be.

We describe some proven activities that will enliven the classroom, but there is no overt pedagogy. Numerous books on reading, writing, and vocabulary methodologies can be found in publishers' catalogs, in university libraries and bookstores, and online. In our earlier writings, we published our research- and application-based recommendations for helping students learn words and expand their reading and writing vocabularies.[4] In the present work, we display the magnificence of words, especially words used well.

Words: The Foundation of Literacy has ten chapters. Chapter 1 is an exploration of the dynamic nature of American English, which welcomes all words and expressions into the fold whether old or new, foreign-born or home-grown. Chapter 2 is a repository of English words and expressions with stories about their origins. It presents a sampling of words from each letter of the alphabet. Our language freely has adopted words from the languages of the world, as is seen in this chapter. Chapter 3 describes how we form new words from existing words or recombinations of their elements. Words are formed through various types of word combining, word shortening, word conversions, and derivations as well as through abbreviations. Chapter 4 addresses the question, "How are words organized in our minds?" As we learn new words, how do we keep them all sorted out? The focus is on the semantic system of English that enables us to mentally store and access the tens of thousands of words we acquire before we enter college.

The abundance of multiple-meaning words in English is the focus of Chapter 5. Many words have two or three meanings (e.g., *lumber, duck, story*), and some words have numerous meanings (e.g., *back, line, down*). Such words are the reason learning English is so difficult. Beginning with a story written entirely with figurative expressions and some informal language, Chapter 6 describes seven types of figurative language: idioms, similes, metaphors, personification, euphemisms, hyperbole, and chiasmus. Figurative language is the expressive use of language in which words are used in nonliteral ways. Proverbs, the subject of Chapter 7, add richness to the language. Proverbs are sayings—whether wise observations about life (e.g., *Experience is the best teacher*) or advisory statements (e.g., *People who live in glass houses shouldn't throw stones*)—that have stood the test of time. Several proverbs are included and defined.

Onomastics, the study of names, forms the basis for Chapter 8. Names of particular persons, places, and things—from residential subdivisions to menu items to hurricanes—are included. Eponyms and toponyms, words whose names come from people (e.g., *Jacuzzi*) and places (e.g., *frankfurter*) are featured. Chapter 9's focus is word play, an important but often overlooked part of the school curriculum. It features more than 200 riddles of the hinky-pinky type (e.g., *What might you call an odd-behaving gobbler? Answer: a quirky turkey*). In the final chapter, we survey a collection of words used in catchphrases and slogans as well as in quotations of lasting significance or humor. Included are predictions from "the experts" that didn't pan out.

In a book on invented languages ranging from *Lingua Ignota* invented in 1150 to *Dritok* invented in 2007, Arika Okrent describes 500 of the 900 known invented languages and concludes: "The history of invented languages is, for the most part, a history of failure."[5] One invented language, *Basic English*, attempted to reduce the English language to 850 words. Basic English failed despite the support of Sir Winston Churchill. As you read *Words: The Foundation of Literacy*, you will see why an 850-word lexicon would never do.

Notes

1. George A. Miller, *The Science of Words* (New York: Scientific American Library, 1996), p. 5.

2. Eve V. Clark, *Cambridge Studies in Linguistics: The Lexicon in Acquisition* (Cambridge, UK: Cambridge University Press, 1993), p. 1.

3. Gerry T. M. Altmann, *The Ascent of Babel: An Exploration of Language, Mind, and Understanding* (Oxford, UK: Oxford University Press, 1997), p. 160.

4. Bonnie Johnson, *Wordworks: Exploring Language Play* (Golden, CO: Fulcrum Publishing, 1999); Dale D. Johnson, *Vocabulary in the Elementary and Middle School* (Needham Heights, MA: Allyn & Bacon, 2001).

5. Arika Okrent, *In the Land of Invented Languages* (New York: Spiegel & Grau, 2009), p. 12.

Our Language

Something Old, Something New

Time flies when you're having fun.
Time's fun when you're having flies.
Time heals all wounds.
Time wounds all heels.
nine to five; twenty-four, seven
time belts
Times Square

American English is a dynamic, spirited, democratic system of communication. All words and expressions are invited to participate in the system whether they are ancient, newly coined, or taken from other languages. Some words and expressions eventually disappear, never to be seen or heard again. Others enter the language and remain, working their way up from slang to "acceptable" English. Some words leave for a while and then reappear with meanings different from their original meanings. Our language is a pulsating mixture that reflects the history, sense of humor, creativity, and technological advances of our people. A brief discussion of the time-related words and sentences above illustrates the richness of American English.

> *Time flies when you're having fun.* "Time flies" was used by the ancient Romans, appeared in English in the Middle Ages, and arrived in America in 1710. The source of "when you're having fun" has been lost, but the versatile expression can be used in a sincere or cynical way. *Time's fun when you're having flies* is an observation from puppeteer Jim Henson's Kermit the Frog.[1]

The comforting *Time heals all wounds* also originated in ancient Rome, and the reassuring *Time wounds all heels* is attributed to the American comedian W. C. Fields.[2]

Nine to five (or 9 to 5) and *twenty-four, seven* (or 24/7) are time-related pairs of numbers used as single words. *Nine to five,* the title of a popular 1980s movie, Broadway musical, and Grammy-winning theme song, has come to mean a routine, somewhat uninspiring job. *Twenty-four, seven,* in use by 1985,[3] is a clever way of stating "around the clock."

Time belts is an obsolete expression. We now call these belts *time zones,*[4] but Americans have many other "belts" in their language, including the *Sun Belt* (the South and Southwest), the *Corn Belt* (several Midwestern states), the *Snow Belt* (states that have heavy snowfall owing to their location near the Great Lakes), and the *Rust Belt* (parts of the upper Midwest and Northeast where heavy industry has disappeared).

Times Square, site of the New Year's Eve ball drop, was named for the *New York Times* newspaper building that was on 43rd Street in Manhattan in the early 1900s. The name has taken on a more contemporary meaning since the advent of the hip-hop culture. *Times Square* is not only a proper noun; in a dictionary of hip-hop terms, it is an adjective that means "fun, exciting."[5]

Words are a part of us. They can relieve anxiety ("He'll make a full recovery"), build up ("You've done a great job"), and tear down ("As usual, your idea is stupid"). Words can inspire a nation ("Ask not what your country can do for you, ask what you can do for your country"). They can amuse ("Never eat in a restaurant that has a skinny chef") and frustrate ("Your flight has been cancelled"). American English is a multimillion-word free-for-all that invites multidisciplinary study.

In the last several years of public schooling in America, the joys and discoveries of working with words have taken a backseat to preparation for standardized test questions. The "teaching for the test" political wave determined, without input from classroom teachers, that word study, if not tested, was not important enough to teach. But teaching students more than quickly forgotten test-prep content is necessary for survival in today's world of reading. Web sites, television programs, magazines, and other media are filled with American English vocabulary that is not found on standardized tests. Here, for example, are just three newspaper headlines that use colorful language:

"Politicians Watch Criminals Pack More Heat" (*New York Times*, January 18, 2010, p. A18).

"Pinch Those Pennies Tighter for Cheapest of the Cheap Contest" (*The Tennessean*, January 31, 2010, p. 1; available online at http:www.tennessean.com).

"Her Daily Grind Just Got Sweeter" (*Newsday*, February 3, 2010, p. A8).

"Be Willing to Make Waves" (*Atlanta Journal-Constitution*, February 14, 2010, p. A21).

An emphasis on "teaching for the test" without addressing the sparkle of a well-turned phrase, the engaging history of words and expressions, and the ever-changing nature of American English can turn the language arts into a rather hollow, dreary endeavor for students and teachers.

American English

In 1813, Thomas Jefferson recommended that Americans develop their own version of the English language more appropriate for our young, democratic nation.[6] Noah Webster was thirteen years ahead of Jefferson's sentiment. At age 42, Webster began to record popular words used by Americans. The word *lengthy*, for example, is an American original and was included in Webster's compilation. As one historian writes of Webster, "Outside his family, nearly everyone who knew him hated him."[7] Webster's bad temperament can be understood when one considers that it took him twenty-eight years to write the 70,000 entries for his *American Dictionary of the English Language.* Webster noted that "the reasons for American English being different than English are simple: As an independent nation, our honor requires us to have a system of our own, in language as well as government."[8]

Long before Webster's feat and Jefferson's recommendation, explorers and colonists were using words learned from Native Americans. Examples include *raccoon, opossum, moose, skunk, pecan,* and *caucus.* The spellings of the words may have been different from modern American spellings, but the meanings are the same. Some words, brought to America from other countries, were modified. In the early 1600s, *corn,* for example, referred to the main grain crop in England—regardless of type of grain. In America, with the preponderance of corn grown by Native Americans, *corn* became specific to the ancestor of our modern corn.[9]

American technology has supplied the world with numerous words from *telephone* to *computer.* American popular culture gave the world *rock and roll, T-shirt,* and *jazz.* American slang contributed *O.K., cool,* and *showbiz* to global speech. The inventiveness of a people and the contributions of immigrants from countries around the world have made American English the vibrant and entertaining language that it is today.

How Our Language Has Changed

There is a disparity of resources in American classrooms. Affluent districts have up-to-date materials; most economically poor classrooms have outdated, meager tools. We taught in one of the poorest schools in America where the third-grade classrooms had only 52-year-old dictionaries for the pupils; and the fourth-grade classrooms, only 49-year-old dictionaries. There was no money to buy more recent books—just money available for test-prep materials. It irks us when we hear some politicians say that money doesn't matter in education. It certainly mattered when it came to having our pupils work with their dictionaries because our language has changed dramatically in the last several decades. In the "New Words Section" of the dictionary the third graders used,[10] the following words, among others, were listed:

ack-ack
alligator
baby sitter
be bop
bobby-soxer
cheeseburger
cover crop
freezer
iron lung
jalopy
new look
soap opera

Ack-ack is defined as the sound of antiaircraft guns and *alligator* as a type of amphibious vehicle that is equipped with weapons. These entries are just two of many war-related "new" words. Others include *airlift, beach head, bombardier, bridgehead, buzz bomb, corvette* (a ship of war), *depth charge, destroyer escort, DP* (displaced persons), *motor torpedo boat, robot bomb, strafe, turret,* and many more. The words mirrored the times. When the dictionary was printed, World War II had just ended; therefore, the entries were deemed important enough for children to know. We might question how essential these entries are for elementary school children in today's classrooms. *Baby sitter, cheeseburger, freezer,* and *soap opera* no longer are "new" words, and the definition of *soap opera,* a "radio serial drama performed on a daytime commercial program chiefly for housewives,"[11] could use some updating. *Be-bop* was a popular type of music during the era, a *bobby-soxer* was a teenage girl, an *iron lung* was a device into which polio patients were put to help them breathe, a *jalopy* was a rundown car or plane, and *new look* referred to, in part, 1947 women's fashions. The "New Words Section" also had several words related to agriculture such as *cover crop* (used to give the soil a rest); *subsurface tillage* (a form of plowing); *trash farming* (a mulching and conservation strategy); *2, 4-D* (kills weeds); and *wilt disease* (plants wilt). During the 1940s, there were more family farms than there are now, so the inclusion of these entries made sense to the dictionary editors of that time. Entries in the outdated dictionaries our pupils were expected to use included words such as *poorhouse* ("a residence for paupers, maintained at public expense") and *raiment* ("Clothing in general; garments").[12] These words rarely are used today unless they are couched in historical text. Words in more recent children's dictionaries such as *air bag, astronaut, condo, contact lens, fast food, mall, software,* and others cannot be found in older editions.

Obsolete Words

Our fourth graders' dictionaries contained numerous words that have been dropped from today's American English. Examples included *hie,* which means "to go quickly," and *hight,* which means "named; called," as in "The knight was hight Gawain." Other words, such as *pshaw,* "an exclamation expressing impatience, contempt, or dislike," were on their way to obsolescence.[13]

Why do words become obsolete? Time marches on, and for some words, there no longer is a need for their existence. The word *boanthropy,* for example, meant "a mental condition in which one thought that he or she was an ox."[14] Oxen are no longer a common sight in the United States, so, to put *boanthropy* in a contemporary dictionary would just take up limited space. In 1977, Susan Kelz Sperling compiled a lengthy list of other words that have become obsolete.[15] Among them are:

acatery	a place where food for royalty was stored
backstress	a baker who is a woman
carked	troubled, uneasy
gundygut	someone who eats in a piggish way
lineseat	a seat used while spinning fibers into thread
mobard	a person with bad manners
pancart	a sign with information for the public
roaky	uncertain, vague
sloomy	a do-nothing, a slug

swarf penny	money paid to those who guard castles
thibble	a utensil for stirring soup
trantles	worthless items
white liver	someone who is not brave

(*Lily livered,* a contemporary expression for *coward,* came from the last of these terms. A white lily has no dark color, and a white liver has no bile. Bile was thought to spawn courage.)

Even though the words above sound odd today, at some point in time they were common in the English language. Wars, new peoples and generations, and the passage of time without frequent use of the words relegated them to obsolescence.

In 1755, Samuel Johnson compiled *A Dictionary of the English Language.* David Crystal selected 4,000 entries from the original *Dictionary* and published them in an anthology.[16] The collection lets us peer back in word-time to twenty-one years before the Declaration of Independence was signed. Many words defined in the *Dictionary* no longer are in use. Among them, in Samuel Johnson's own words, are:

bootcatcher	The person whose business at an inn is to pull off the boots of passengers.
ferula	An instrument of correction with which young scholars are beaten on the hand; so named because anciently the stalks of fennel were used for this purpose.
mouthfriend	One who professes friendship without intending it.
penner	A writer.
scambler	A bold intruder upon one's generosity or table.

Technological advances account for many word deaths—or near deaths. The word *keypunching* is heard or seen only in a historical sense. It referred to the process of making small holes with a machine in a card so that a large computer could "read" the card. *Record players*, which used *needles* to play sound, also had been relegated to the historical word pile, but in recent years, vinyl LPs have been making a comeback.

The history of words teaches us that we cannot, however, be premature in announcing the death of some words. In 1755, Samuel Johnson noted that *chivalrous, ignore, jeopardy,* and *remediate* were not in use.[17] We can ignore that declaration.

Old Words Still in Use

Some of our most common, everyday words are hundreds of years old. The preposition *in* dates from the 700s. *Hill* can be traced to 1175. Although some of the spellings have changed throughout the years, we still use many old words and their meanings. Below are other common words and their approximate dates of origin.[18]

ballot	1549
candle	before 1160
et cetera	1150
flower (noun)	before 1200
fun	before 1325
lettuce	1300s
organize	1413
pollution	1300s
potato	1565
rat	1100
sparkle	1338

Many of the words and phrases we use today were entries in Samuel Johnson's 1755 *Dictionary.* Their meanings have not changed since Johnson compiled his work. These include *certain, comedian, encore, foolhardy, giggle, hammock, hide and seek, incognito, inconspicuous, vacuum, volcano,* and *yacht.*

Word Meanings That Have Returned

Some word meanings leave the language for a while and reappear years later. Owing to their lengthy absence, they seem fresh upon their return.

This is particularly true of word meanings used by America's youth, who are impressively inventive with language. Thomas Dalzell has compiled a list of words used by college students around 1900.[19] *Drink* (a river, stream), *freak* (as in *control freak*), and *nail* (to do well on something) are from that era. The meanings may have come and gone in popularity, but even today, more than a century later, most people can understand the following sentences:

She threw a large branch into the *drink.*
The twins are computer *freaks.*
I *nailed* that exam.

Some words are thought to be relatively current, but they have been in use for a long time. Words for *money* such as *dough, loot,* and *dead presidents* can be traced to 1851, 1928, and 1944, respectively. To give the *lowdown* on something dates back to 1908, and *homeboy* and *homegirl* were part of the vocabulary in 1899.[20]

Word Meanings That Have Changed Completely

Perhaps no word's meaning has changed more than that of *geek.* Rosemarie Ostler notes that *geek* used to be a carnival word "for someone whose act consisted of biting the heads off live chickens and snakes."[21] The word evolved with a less hideous definition in the 1980s. During that time, a *geek* referred to a person who usually was adept with computers but was somewhat awkward socially. *Geek* has since taken on a favorable meaning. Today's *geek* is still smart and technologically savvy (and probably worth some money) but, in most circles, is no longer a social isolate.

Another word whose meaning has done an about-face is *bully.* In the 1500s, *bully* referred to a good, kind person. As Adrian Room explains,[22] some of Shakespeare's works use the original meaning of the word, and this can cause confusion for today's readers.

Punk is a Native American word that entered American English in 1618. It originally meant corn that had been cooked too long. Over the years, its meaning changed to "sticks used to start a fire" (early 1800s), "not worth a lot" (1889), "a young lawbreaker" (1918–1945), and, in the 1970s, "associated with a type of music" (e.g., *punk rocker*).[23]

Sol Steinmetz and Barbara Ann Kipfer point out that "*fabulous* is a word that once meant 'based on or pertaining to a fable.' It came to mean 'incredible' or 'marvelous' since those adjectives could describe fables." They also note that the original meaning of *meticulous* was "fearful, timid," and that *naughty* originally meant "having nothing, needy."[24]

In the early 1800s, the wholly American word *airline* originally meant "in a direct line," as in "Pat made an *airline* to the cookies." By the mid-1800s, *airline* was used by the railroads to describe a direct route, and by the early 1900s, the word had taken on its current meaning.[25]

Chuckle used to mean "to laugh loudly and in a spirited way," *nosy* meant "to have a huge nose," and *glimmer* referred to a bright light rather than to a faint or dim light. During the 1960s, before personal computers became commonplace, one meaning of *crash* was "to sleep," a common meaning of *plastic* was "fake" or "phony," and *hood* was short for *hoodlum.* There are entire dictionaries of words whose meanings have changed throughout the ages.[26]

Samuel Johnson's 1755 *Dictionary* contains numerous words whose meanings have changed.[27] Among these are:

glossary	A dictionary of obscure or antiquated words.
go-cart	A machine in which children are inclosed [*sic*] to teach them to walk, and which they push forward without danger of falling.
lunch, luncheon	As much food as one's hand can hold.
recipe	A medical prescription.

Words That Have Become "Respectable"

Slang has been defined as "an informal, nonstandard, nontechnical vocabulary composed chiefly of novel-sounding synonyms for standard words and phrases."[28] As time passes, some words and expressions "move up" from slang status. *Dwindle, fretful, fireworks,* and *hubbub,* for example, were considered slang when Shakespeare used them.[29]

As Peter Farb points out, "Occasionally some slang words—like *joke, fad, boom, crank,* and *slump*—become respectable items in the vocabulary." Paul Dickson similarly notes that "English words as diverse as *snide, hold up, nice* (as in '*nice work*'), *bogus, strenuous, clumsy,* and *spurious* were regarded as slang not that long ago."[30] Numerous words and expressions that were slang when they were coined now are established in American English. Examples include *alibi, baby boomer, bore* (referring to a person), *bouncer* (an evictor), *crowd* (a large group of people), *crunch* (as in *time crunch*), *curveball, gooey, graffiti, groggy,* and *iffy.*[31] *Bellhop* and *quiz* also were slang,[32] and as Steinmetz and Kipfer point out, "*accountable, donate, enthused, practitioner, presidential,* and *reliable* were roundly condemned and ridiculed by influential critics of the late 19th and early 20th centuries."[33]

"In-Between" Words

Some words and expressions, although remarkably old, still teeter on the boundary between established vocabulary and slang. We have coined the term *in-betweens* for them. No one can determine when the in-betweens move from one category to the other. They are not outrageous or offensive words, but they are words that most speakers or writers would not select for formal use.

Many in-between words and expressions have been in use for a long time. *Above-board,* for example, is an entry in Samuel Johnson's 1755 *Dictionary.* The definition was "In open sight; without artifice or trick. A figurative expression, borrowed from gamesters, who, when they put their hands under the table, are changing their cards."[34] Johnson explains in the entry that *above-board* "is used only in familiar language." It remains an in-between to this day. Following are some other examples of old in-betweens:[35]

chicken feed—1836
lowlife—1766

> *cranky*—1812
> *mouthpiece* (lawyer)—1857
> *cushy*—1915
> *mushy* (too sentimental)—1839
> *firebug*—1872
> *night owl*—1847
> *flunk*—1823
> *oodles* (a large quantity)—early 1900s

In-betweens are often clever and sometimes irreverent. The American business world gave us such in-betweens as *paper pusher* (someone whose job involves a lot of paperwork) and *pink slip* (a notification that one's job is terminated). *Gofer* (someone who does many small tasks for another) and *sleeper* (a show that is a surprising hit) come from the entertainment world. *Road hog, road rage,* and *gridlock* come from navigating a vehicle in heavy traffic.

Many in-betweens came from wars in which Americans were involved. For example, *deadbeat* and *greenback* (dollar bill) were used during the Civil War; *basketcase, chow, foxhole,* and *hush hush* (something to be kept quiet) are from World War I; *brass* (high-ranking officers), *dry run, goobledygook* (bureaucratic jibberish), *goof up, near miss,* and *on target* are from World War II; *chopper* (helicopter) is from the Korean War; and *care package* is from the Vietnam War.[36] Research suggests that "even though some words and phrases might have originated earlier, slang from wars became better known simply because so many Americans were engaged, one way or the other, in the wars."[37]

Some in-between words and expressions rhyme. Examples include *fender bender, local yokel, wear and tear,* and *wheeler dealer.* Some in-betweens repeat a word: *neck-and-neck, a no-no, out-and-out, so-so,* and *on the up-and-up.* Other in-betweens change a letter or two: *chitchat, flip-flop, rinky dink, tip-top, dilly dally,* and *wishy-washy.* All of these expressions are called *reduplicatives* and are discussed in Chapter 3.

It is not difficult to locate words and expressions that entered the language as slang but died a quick, merciful death. Examples include *ham-*

and-egger (an ordinary individual), *to woof* (to talk), *boo* (really good), *zorch* (excellent), *road dog* (a best friend), and *circle of death* (a bad pizza).[38]

Why do some slang words and expressions "move up" whereas others retain their slang status, creep up to "in-betweens," or rapidly disappear? Common sense tells us that for a word or expression to become part of established American English, it must be used repeatedly and it must be seen and heard in the media—preferably in the influential media. A slang term frequently used by well-known television personalities and seen many times online or in hard copies of the *New York Times*, for example, has a better chance of becoming "respectable" than if the term were used verbally by only a small group of people. Even as this sentence is being written, some group somewhere is using a slang term that might someday enter established American English. Examples include *marinate* (to consider), *overstand* (to really understand), and *hair don't* (a bad hairstyle).[39]

New Words

Every moment that humans are mingling, exploring, or inventing, there is a possibility that a new word will emerge. Perhaps the word will come from an urban street corner or a rural agricultural discovery or an office in midtown Manhattan. Whenever it makes its debut, it has a long road ahead of it to become widely used. Allan Metcalf notes that "it takes about two generations to know for sure whether a word will be a permanent addition to the vocabulary."[40] Terms such as *fast food* (1954), *software* (1959), and *carpool* (1962) now seem to be safe bets—that is, unless some other term or technology replaces their usefulness or their meanings change. As Jonathan Evan Lighter points out, "No word is utterly stable."[41]

The term *neologism* refers to a new word or a new meaning for an established word. For example, *second-hand speech* was a neologism in 2001.[42] It means the overheard conversations of cellphone users. A definition of *mouse* was a neologism when its meaning shifted from "small rodent" to include, in 1965, "computer part." *Surf* became a neologism in 1993 when it was used as an Internet term rather than just a word for riding big waves of water.

The American Dialect Society has been keeping an eye on new words for many years. Since 1990, the Society began voting on Words of the Year. The 2008 Word of the Year was *bailout,* referring to "the rescue by the government of companies on the brink of failure, including large players in the banking industry."[43] Nominations for the 2007 Words of the Year included *bacn* and *wrap rage* in the Most Useful category. *Bacn* refers to e-mail that automatically appears because the recipient agreed to receive it. The term, because of its food-category closeness to *spam,* implies that the recipient is not particularly pleased when the *bacn* arrives. *Wrap rage* means to get upset from trying to open securely sealed packaging.[44] Neither nominee won. The winner was *subprime* (in the Real Estate category); it refers to unwise property loans. In 2006, *plutoed* was named the Word of the Year. To *pluto* is "to demote or devalue someone or something, as happened to the former planet Pluto when the General Assembly of the International Astronomical Union decided Pluto no longer met its definition of a planet."[45] Today, the seldom-used *plutoed* illustrates how difficult it is to predict a word's staying power. Some of the Society's choices are still in common use. These include *podcast* (2005 Most Useful), *blog* (2002 Most Likely to Succeed), *google* (verb, 2002 Most Useful), the prefix *e-* as in *e-mail* (1998 Word of the Year), *cyber* and *morph* (1994 Words of the Year), *snail mail* (1992 Most Likely to Succeed), and *politically correct* (1990 Most Outrageous). It is clear that several of the words grew from computer technology, and that one of the terms, *politically correct*, is no longer considered "outrageous."

Some of the American Dialect Society's choices for Words of the Year under a variety of categories have slipped from common usage.[46] Examples include *dot bomb* (a dot com that is no longer in business, 2002 Most Creative) and *prairie dogging* (looking over a cubicle while at work, 1997 Most Original).

In 2000, the American Dialect Society selected *web* as the "Word of the 1990s Decade" and *jazz* as the "Word of the Twentieth Century." Its selection for "Word of the Past Millennium" was *she.* The Society explained:

Before the year 1000, there was no **she** in English; just **heo**, which singular females had to share with plurals of all [i.e., both] genders because it meant **they** as well. In the twelfth century, however, **she** appeared, and **she** has been with us ever since. **She** may derive from the Old English feminine demonstrative pronoun **seo** or **sio**, or from Viking invasions.[47]

Merriam-Webster OnLine listed some of the new words included in its "2006 update of *Merriam-Webster's Collegiate® Dictionary, Eleventh Edition*."[48] Words such as *spyware* (monitoring computer activities without a user's consent) and *sandwich generation* (people taking care of their own parents and their own children) are still in use. Others such as *mouse potato* (someone who spends a lot of time on a computer) might be destined for the word storage bin.

The Random House "Words@Random" Web site lists words that entered our language since the 1940s.[49] New words from the 1940s that we still use include *fax, quiz show, test drive*, and *TV*. *Jet plane* has been shortened to *jet*, and a *flying saucer* is now known as a *UFO* (which entered the language in 1953).[50]

Brainstorming, car wash, hash browns, and *skydiving* are "new" words from the 1950s that still are used. The 1950s term *junk mail* is teetering on formal usage, but *weirdo* is an in-between. The 1960s gave us *jet lag, microwave oven, sitcom, trendy*, and the in-between *glitch*. *Infomercial, Silicon Valley, trail mix*, and the in-between *bean counter* are from the 1970s. New words and phrases from the 1980s include *ATM* (automated-teller machine), *channel surf, voice mail*, and the in-betweens *mall rat* and *wannabe*. *Designated driver, personal trainer*, and *Web site* entered the language in the 1990s.

New Words for Newcomers

If we move from one part of the country to another, it does not take long before we encounter words and expressions that are unfamiliar to us. Metcalf notes that large, busy roads are called by various names in different parts of the country.[51] In some West Coast areas, they are *freeways*,

in several Midwestern states they are *interstates* or *tollroads* (e.g., the Indiana Tollroad), and in the metro New York City area they are *turnpikes*
(e.g., the New Jersey Turnpike), *expressways* (e.g., the Long Island Ex-
pressway), and *parkways* (e.g., the Southern State Parkway). Bostonians
sometimes put *jimmies* on ice cream. So do Wisconsinites, but they call
them *sprinkles.* Our New York students tell us that they have to wait *on
line* for something, but students in other regions of the country whom
we have taught have waited *in line.* Our New York students *schlep* stacks
of books, our former Louisiana students *toted* the books, and our students in the Midwest *lugged* the books. Our former Wisconsin students
drank *pop,* our New York students drink *soda. Y'all, you guys,* and *youse
guys* mean the same thing. A Louisiana student told us that *all y'all* was
meant for groups larger than twenty people and that the possessive form
is *all y'allses',* but she might have been pulling our Yankee legs.

A Brief Word-Walk Through History from the 1700s to the Twenty-First Century

Words arise from human activities and define human activities. Below is
a sampling of words that help to define who we are and where we are
headed.[52] The date listed is the date that the word appeared in print. You
will note that some of the words are surprisingly old.

1785	*parachute*
1789	*immigrant*
1808	*rowdy*
1819	*tabloid*
1825	*blizzard*
1845	*chicken pot pie*
1850	*aircraft*
1859	*acid rain*
1865	*commuter*
1873	*ecology*
1883	*skyscraper*

1895	*modern art*
1899	*aspirin*
1900	*escalator*
1902	*birthday card*
1917	*traffic jam*
1929	*greenhouse effect, polyester*
1933	*supermarket*
1953	*fish sticks*
1960	*theme park*
1961	*area code*
1962	*carpool, database, trendy*
1964	*prime time, sitcom*
1966	*designer* (adjective), *number cruncher*
1967	*bumper sticker, rip off*
1969	*jet lag, ego-trip*
1973	*salad bars*
1977	*user friendly*
1979	*couch potato, downsize*
1980	*download, soundbite*
1982	*e-mail, text messaging*
1994	*Web site, morph*
2004	*red states, blue states, purple states*
2006	*YouTube*
2007	*subprime*
2008	*bailout* (i.e., the U.S. government's supplying funds to cash-poor corporations)

Instructional Activity 1.1

1. Select a decade (e.g., the 1960s, the 1980s, or the last ten years) in American history. List words that are representative of that era.
2. Compile a list of words that sprang from the invention of the automobile, commercial air travel, and widespread computer usage.

3. In a group, create two or three neologisms. In addition to the definitions, include the parts of speech and use the neologisms in the same paragraph.
4. Look and listen for new words, and list suggestions for next year's "Word of the Year."

1.1

Notes

1. Gregory Y. Titelman, *Random House Dictionary of Popular Proverbs and Sayings* (New York: Random House, 1996); Mardy Grothe, *Never Let a Fool Kiss You or a Kiss Fool You: Chiasmus and a World of Quotations That Say What They Mean and Mean What They Say* (New York: Viking, 1999).

2. William Morris and Mary Morris, *Morris Dictionary of Word and Phrase Origins*, 2nd ed. (New York: HarperCollins, 1977 [reprinted in 1988]).

3. Allan A. Metcalf, *How We Talk: American Regional English Today* (Boston: Houghton Mifflin, 2000).

4. David K. Barnhart and Allan A. Metcalf, *America in So Many Words: Words That Have Shaped America* (Boston: Houghton Mifflin, 1997).

5. Alonzo Westbrook, *Hip Hoptionary: The Dictionary of Hip Hop Terminology* (New York: Broadway Books, 2002), p. 141.

6. Einar Haugen, "Short History of the English Language," in *The Barnhart Concise Dictionary of Etymology*, ed. Robert K. Barnhart, xvii–xxi (New York: HarperCollins, 1995).

7. Ibid., p. 2.

8. Quoted in Stuart Berg Flexner and Anne H. Soukhanov, *Speaking Freely: A Guided Tour of American English from Plymouth Rock to Silicon Valley* (New York: Oxford University Press, 1997), p. 11.

9. Flexner and Soukhanov, *Speaking Freely*; Barnhart and Metcalf, *America in So Many Words*.

10. G. & C. Merriam Company, *Webster's Elementary Dictionary: A Dictionary for Boys and Girls* (New York: American Book Company, 1945 [reprinted in 1949]).

11. Ibid., p. xix.

12. Ibid., pp. 472, 502.

13. E. L. Thorndike and Clarence L. Barnhart, *Thorndike Barnhart Beginning Dictionary* (Chicago: Scott, Foresman and Company, 1952), pp. 304, 459.

14. Bonnie Johnson, *Wordworks: Exploring Language Play* (Golden, CO: Fulcrum Publishing, 1999), p. 120.

15. Susan Kelz Sperling, *Poplollies & Bellibones: A Celebration of Lost Words* (Old Saybrook, CT: Konecky & Konecky, 1977).

16. David Crystal, *A Dictionary of the English Language: An Anthology.* (New York: Penguin, 2005), pp. 101, 239, 387, 428, 505.

17. Ibid., p. xii.

18. Robert K. Barnhart, ed., *The Barnhart Concise Dictionary of Etymology* (New York: HarperCollins, 1995).

19. Thomas Dalzell, *Flappers 2 Rappers: American Youth Slang* (Springfield, MA: Merriam-Webster, 1996).

20. Jonathan Evan Lighter, ed., *Random House Historical Dictionary of American Slang*, vol. 1 (New York: Random House, 1994); Jonathan Evan Lighter, ed., *Random House Historical Dictionary of American Slang*, vol. 2 (New York: Random House, 1997).

21. Rosemarie Ostler, *Dewdroppers, Waldos, and Slackers: A Decade-by-Decade Guide to the Vanishing Vocabulary of the Twentieth Century* (Oxford, UK: Oxford University Press, 2003), p. xii.

22. Adrian Room, *NTC's Dictionary of Changes in Meanings* (Lincolnwood, IL: National Textbook Company, 1991).

23. Barnhart, *The Barnhart Concise Dictionary of Etymology.*

24. Sol Steinmetz and Barbara Ann Kipfer, *The Life of Language* (New York: Random House Reference, 2006), pp. 105, 108.

25. Jeffrey McQuain, *Home-Grown English: How Americans Invented Themselves and Their Language* (New York: Random House, 1999).

26. Room, *NTC's Dictionary of Changes in Meanings.*

27. Crystal, *A Dictionary of the English Language*, pp. 272, 273, 359, 475.

28. Lighter, *Random House Historical Dictionary of American Slang*, vol. 1, p. xi.

29. Paul Dixon, *Slang! Topic-by-Topic Dictionary of Contemporary American Lingoes* (New York: Pocket Books, 1990).

30. Peter Farb, *Word Play: What Happens When People Talk* (New York: Alfred A. Knopf, 1973); Dickson, *Slang! Topic-by-Topic Dictionary*, p. xiv.

31. Johnson, *Wordworks.*

32. Howard Richler, *A Bawdy Language* (New York: Stoddart, 1998).

33. Steinmetz and Kipfer, *The Life of Language*, p. 217.

34. Crystal, *A Dictionary of the English Language*, p. 47.

35. Lighter, *Random House Historical Dictionary of American Slang*, vol. 1; Dalzell, *Flappers 2 Rappers.*

36. Christine Ammer, *Fighting Words: From War, Rebellion, and Other Combative Capers* (Lincolnwood, IL: NTC Publishing Group, 1989 [reprinted in 1999]); Dalzell, *Flappers 2 Rappers.*

37. Johnson, *Wordworks*, p. 72.

38. Dalzell, *Flappers 2 Rappers*; Ronald L. Partin, *The Social Studies Teacher's Book of Lists* (Englewood Cliffs, NJ: Prentice-Hall, 1992).

39. Alonzo Westbrook, *Hip Hoptionary: The Dictionary of Hip Hop Terminology* (New York: Broadway Books, 2002).

40. Metcalf, *How We Talk*, p. 2.

41. Quoted in Hugh Rawson, "Slang: An Interview with J. E. Lighter," *American Heritage*, October 2003, 72.

42. American Dialect Society, "*Plutoed*" Voted 2006 Word of the Year by American Dialect Society, 2007, http://www.americandialect.org/Word-of-the-year_2006.pdf.

43. American Dialect Society, American Dialect Society 2008 Word of the Year Is "Bailout," 2009, http://www.americandialect.org/index.php/amerdial/categories/C178.

44. American Dialect Society, American Dialect Society 2007 Words of the Year Nominations, 2008, http://www.americandialect.org/2007.WOTY.nominations.pdf.

45. American Dialect Society, 2007, p. 1.

46. Ibid.

47. American Dialect Society, 1999 Words of the Year, Word of the 1990s, Word of the 20th Century, Word of the Millennium, 2000, p. 1, http://www.americandialect.org/index.ph/amerdial/1999_word_of_the_year.

48. Merriam-Webster OnLine, New Words, 2008, http://www.merriam-webster.com/info/new_words.htm.

49. Random House, Words@Random, New Words: Sixty Years of New Words, 2008, http://www.randomhouse.com/words/newwords/.

50. Allan A. Metcalf, *Predicting New Words: The Secrets of Their Success* (New York: Houghton Mifflin, 2002).

51. Metcalf, *How We Talk.*

52. Barnhart and Metcalf, *America in So Many Words*; Flexner and Soukhanov, *Speaking Freely*; American Dialect Society, 2006; American Dialect Society, 2007; John Ayto, *A Century of New Words* (Oxford, UK: Oxford University Press, 1999 [reprinted in 2006 and 2007]).

2

Origins

Every Word and Expression Has a Story

The zipper on the freelancer's hoodie was broken. "I wish they made these things with Velcro," he groused as he leaned into the bitter wind.

The dates of origin of the twenty-two different words above range from 950 to 1993. According to *The Barnhart Concise Dictionary of Etymology*),[1] *the, on, was, things, he, into,* and *wind* had appeared in Old English, the earliest period of the language, by the year 950. We can surmise that these words came into existence out of the need to communicate. Prior to their introduction into English, other utterances and gestures had to suffice. By 1250, *make, these, as,* and *leaned* had appeared, as did the borrowed word *they* (from Scandinavia) and *I* (originally *ic* and then *i*). Robert Barnhart points out that *I* became written in the upper case so that it would stand out in handwritten manuscripts.[2] *Wish, with* (meaning "composed of"), and *bitter* (as related to cold weather) were in use between 1150 and 1349. *Broke* (meaning "not functioning properly") was in use by the 1500s, although other meanings of the word, such as "to break a horse," were in use much earlier.

The word *freelancer,* which refers to one who is self-employed, originated in the Middle Ages when some knights were the equivalent of contemporary mercenary soldiers. Rather than fighting for one royal ruler, freelancers carried their spearlike lances from locale to locale to protect—for a price—whoever needed them. *Freelancer* became commonly used after the publication in 1819 of *Ivanhoe,* a work of historical fiction set in medieval days, by Sir Walter Scott, who used the word in the book.[3] Although the noun *grouse* (i.e., a large, reddish-brown bird) entered English before 1550, the verb *grouse* (i.e., to complain, grumble) was not in use until the late 1800s. No one knows for certain the origin of either the noun or verb form of *grouse,* but the verb form is thought to have come from slang used by British soldiers.[4]

The word *zipper* is an American word that entered English in 1925. It originally was a trademark of the B. F. Goodrich Company, and the company's founder, Benjamin Franklin Goodrich, is credited with coining the word. *Zip* was already in the language (noun, 1875; verb, 1852) to describe a quick movement. Goodrich created *zipper* to describe the sound made when he zipped up his boots. Goodrich did not invent the zipper. That honor goes to Whitcomb Judson, who lived in Chicago and designed the device, called a *clasp-locker,* in 1893. Early zippers were something of a flop. They had to be removed from an article of clothing before washing because the metal in the zipper would rust if it got wet. Then the zipper would have to be sewn back into the garment. Early zippers also jammed a lot, and that problem still does not seem to have been solved.[5]

One solution to zippers that jammed was the Swiss invention of *Velcro* in the mid-1950s by George de Mestral. The material, composed of little hooks and eyes, was inspired by the stubborn burs that stuck to de Mestral's clothing and dog. The word *Velcro* is a blend of *velour* and *crochet*.[6] In most references to the material, *Velcro* is capitalized because it is a trademark. *Zipper*, as mentioned above, also is a trademark and should be capitalized. The word, however, has fallen into *genericide*.[7] Genericide is what happens when a trade name becomes so successful that it comes into use as a generic term. Regardless of the manufacturer, *zipper* represents all zippers. Other former trade names that have become the victims of genericide are *band-aid, granola,* and *thermos.*

Hoodie, a usually long-sleeved garment with an attached hood, is a recent addition to American English. Although undoubtedly heard in urban neighborhoods before it was seen in print, the word first appeared in a *New York Times* article in 1993.[8]

The zipper on the freelancer's hoodie was broken. "I wish they made these things with Velcro," he groused as he leaned into the bitter wind. One twenty-five-word sentence with twenty-two different words spans a history of more than 1,000 years in their origins.

Etymology and Word Origins

There is a difference between etymology and word origins. As Tom McArthur explains, "Whereas scholarly dictionaries of etymology describe the histories of many thousands of words in dense entries with often formidable arrays of abbreviations and parentheses, books and articles on word origins tend to discuss a more limited range of words whose unusual 'stories' are often described in an expansive and relaxed style."[9] One entry, the word *joy,* from *The Oxford Dictionary of English Etymology*, illustrates McArthur's point:

> **joy** dʒoi pleasurable emotion; state of happiness. XIII.–OF. *joie, joye* (mod. *joie*) = Pr. *joia,* Sp. *joya,* It. *gioia* :–Rom. **gaudia,* fem. for L. *gaudia,* pl. of *gaudium* joy (whence Pr. *joi*), f. *gaud re.* So **joy** vb. †rejoice XIII (Cursor M.); †ENJOY XIV.–OF. *jo r* (mod. *jouir*) = Pr. *gaudir* :– Rom. **gaud re,* for L. *gaud re* rejoice, f. **gawedh-*(cf. synon. Gr. *g theîn,*

f. *g eth-). So **joy** ANCE. XVI (Spenser). **joy** OUS. XIV.–AN. *joyous,* OF. *joios* (mod. *joyeux*).[10]

It takes a great deal of flipping to pronunciation guides and special symbol keys to interpret nearly all of the entries in etymological dictionaries, and this can take the "joy" out of word study for most individuals who are not etymological scholars. We will therefore, in this chapter, discuss only word origins. A word of caution is in order when conducting research on the origins of words. Some resources have engaging tales of how some words originated, but the stories cannot be verified by scholars in the field. *Blimp, penguin,* and *snooze* are examples.[11] In the following section, we have found support for each origin in at least two of the works cited in the corresponding endnote.

A Sampling of Word Origins

Here is a sampling of word origins, two for each letter of the alphabet.[12]

alphabet	This word comes from the first two letters of the Greek alphabet, *alpha* and *beta*. There was some controversy about using the word *alphabet* in the 1400s, when it was introduced to English. Some scholars did not want to be copycats and proposed that it be called the *ABC*. They even coined a new word for it: *absey*. The *ABC* proponents didn't completely win the day, but we still ask young children if they know their *ABC*s.
astronaut	The first *astronauts* were selected in 1959. The word *astronaut*, however, entered English in 1929. It was formed from the Greek *astro* (outer space) and *naút s* (sailor). A fictional space vehicle by the name of *Astronaut* can be traced to the late 1800s.
berserk	During the Middle Ages, some Vikings would dress in *berserkers* (*bear skins* in English) instead of the

usual armor. According to battle legends, these warriors, named for the skins that they wore, growled like bears and behaved bravely.

blockbuster   The contemporary usage of this word refers to a wildly successful book, film, or other type of entertainment. *Blockbuster* originated during World War II, when it had little to do with entertainment. It referred to a powerful bomb that could flatten blocks of a city.

cobweb   In the early 1300s, *coppe* meant "spider." Over the years, the spelling went from *coppe* to *cop* and, by the time William Shakespeare used it, the *coppeweb* had become *cobweb*.

crowbar   Although this tool was in use during the 1300s, Americans coined the word in the mid-1700s. They thought that one end of the tool looked like a crow's beak and the other end resembled a crow's foot.

dandelion   This pesky weed with the attractive yellow flower is from the French *dent de lion* which means "lion's tooth." Some word historians believe that the plant is so named because its jagged leaves resemble lions' teeth. Others think that the name refers to the long root of the plant.

dynamite   Alfred Nobel (1833–1896), the Swedish chemist for whom the Nobel Prizes are named, invented dynamite and gave the explosive its name. The word comes from the Greek *dunamis* (power, force) and the suffix *-it* (*-ite* in English).

electric   What would seem to be a relatively new word in English is centuries old. Ancient Greeks found that when amber, a hard resin, was rubbed, it attracted lightweight material. The Greek word for amber was *electron*. In England in the 1600s, William Gilbert conducted experiments using amber to generate static and referred to the phenomenon as *electricus*, the base for the word *electricity*.

escape
This word is from the Latin *ex-* (out) and *cappa* (cape). In the Middle Ages, a person in someone's clutches could slip out of his cape and make a get-away.

fib
A falsehood that is not too serious got its name in the early 1600s when it was called a *fibble-fable*. During those times, a *fable* was a lie but a *fibble-fable* was an silly untruth that would not harm anyone. *Fib* is a clipping of *fibble-fable*.

flunk
An American original, *flunk* entered our language in 1823. The word was slang first used in a Yale College (now University) publication. Some etymologists believe that it is a variation of the mid-1700s British university slang *funk*, which meant "to evade."

gladiator
This word comes from *gladius*, the Latin word for "sword." Gladiators, though usually criminals or slaves, were skilled swordsmen.

gridlock
City streets that crisscross can be viewed as a grid. When there is no smooth traffic flow on these intersecting streets, the grid is "locked," according to traffic engineers. This American word appeared in 1980 and now refers to any severe traffic snarl.

hobby
Hobby is a clipping of *hobby horse* (a child's "rocking horse"). Children ride the horse for amusement, and a hobby is intended to amuse the hobbyist.

honcho
This word became popularized by soldiers returning from Japan after World War II. It is from the Japanese *hanch*, which meant "group leader." *Head honcho* is a familiar American term for a person in charge of something.

iceberg
Iceberg entered English in 1774 and came from the Dutch *ijsberg*, which means "ice mountain." *The tip*

of the iceberg, which refers to a small part of what really exists, entered English much later—in 1963.

impasse
: This word comes from French and literally means a thoroughfare with no outlet. *Impasse* often is used during contract disputes when labor and management cannot agree on one or more issues.

jeans
: In the mid-1500s, *jean* was a type of cloth made in the Italian city of *Gene* or *Jene*. Today we refer to the city as *Genoa*. The plural, *jeans*, entered English in 1843.

jersey
: Some people wear a football *jersey* with their *jeans*. In the 1500s, the island of Jersey, the largest island in the English Channel, was known for its production of knitted garments. *Jersey* still is one kind of knitted material as well as a type of pullover.

kangaroo
: In 1770, while repairing damage to his ship in Australia, British explorer Captain James Cook asked the locals the name of a large animal that he had never seen before. They replied that it was a *gangurru*. Cook recorded this as *kangooroo*. What Cook saw was just one type of kangaroo. There are more than fifty species of the animal, but whether Cook knew this, we do not know.

kaleidoscope
: Sir David Brewster, a Scottish scientist, invented and named this toy made of mirrors and colored shapes in 1817. The word comes from the Greek *kalós* (beautiful) + *eidos* (form) + *skopos* (watcher of beautiful shapes). Another meaning of *kaleidoscope*, that of shifting scenes, entered English in 1819.

laser
: *Laser* comes from *l(ight) a(mplification by the) s(timulated) e(mission of) r(adiation)*. The acronym, coined in 1960, is a relative newcomer to English.

lima bean
: This nutritious bean came from Lima, Peru, and was brought to Europe by Spanish explorers. *Lima bean*

entered English in 1756. The tasty legume is called a *butter bean* in some parts of the United States.

marshmallow
Evenings around campfires are not complete without this sticky treat. The word comes from an herb, the *marsh mallow*, which was used in Middle Ages for medicinal purposes.

moonlighting
Today, to *moonlight* means to have a job in addition to one's full-time job. Securing a second job is admirable, but the original meaning of the word came from seafarers who smuggled illegal goods during the evening hours.

nachos
Not all etymologists agree, but the source of these hot tortilla chips with cheese and toppings appears to be a Mexican restaurant employee whose name was Ignacio Anaya. Ignacio's nickname was *Nacho.* The Tex-Mex appetizer was first concocted in 1943.

noun
The word *noun* is recorded in English as early as 1398. It is from the Latin *nomēn*, which means "name."

octopus
The name for this sea creature with eight arms comes from the Greek *okt* (eight) + *pous* (foot). Octopus is tasty, but most chefs recommend precooking the meat as it can be tough.

October
This autumn month's name is from the Latin *oct* (eight). In the ancient Roman calendar, the year began with March, so October was the eighth month.

piano
Piano is a clipping of the Italian *piano e forte* (soft and loud). Before the piano's invention, harpsichords were used, but they were too soft to hear in concert halls. In 1709, Italian Bartolomeo Christoforo constructed the first piano, which could emit both loud and soft sounds.

poodle
Poodle comes from the German *pudeln* (to splash in water) + *hund* (dog). The poodle was once used by hunters to retrieve waterbirds.

quack	The imitative sound of a duck entered English in the early 1600s, but the *quack* that refers to a bad doctor is a clipping of *quacksalver*, which in Dutch means "to brag about and try to sell one's salves or ointments."
quiche	Often referred to as *quiche Lorraine*, this egg-and-cream mixture in a crust comes from Lorraine, a part of France that borders Germany. Both languages are spoken in this region, and the French inhabitants coined *quiche* from the German *Küche* (little cake).
rhinestone	This word came from the city of Strasbourg, a French city on the Rhine River, where rock crystals were found. The crystals resembled diamonds. Today the word is used for diamond imitations made from a variety of materials.
robot	*Robot* first appeared in a Czech play, *R. U. R.* (Rossum's Universal Robots), in 1923. The word came from the Czech *robata*, which means *forced labor*.
spa	This word comes from the resort town Spa (in eastern Belgium), which, since the 1500s, has been known for its curative waters. Today the word is used to describe places that offer health and grooming programs.
stigma	In the late 1500s, this word, from the Greek *stigma*, meant an intentional mark made on the skin of a slave or criminal. By the early 1600s, the word meant social shame or disgrace.
town	The word *tūn* originally meant "an enclosure." Centuries ago, people clustered together for safety's sake. They would build hedges or fences to keep animals and undesirables out of an area. By the Middle Ages, these hedges or fences were replaced by walls. In the 1300s, the word entered English as *toun*.
T-shirt	This American word came from the shape of the garment, which when spread out, resembles the letter *T*. It entered our language in 1919.

umbrella	From Latin and then Italian, meaning "little shadow" or "little shade," *umbrella* originally referred to a device used to protect people from the sun.
utopia	In 1516, Sir Thomas More wrote a book with this title. The word is formed from the Greek *ou* + *tópos* (no place). Although *Utopia* originally referred to an island in More's work, by the early 1600s it meant a perfect place. Today the word also is used somewhat sarcastically to mean something that cannot be attained.
valedictorian	The top academic student is given this title, which comes from the Latin for "to say farewell." It was first used by Harvard College (now University) in 1759.
vermicelli	The origin of this long, thin pasta's name comes from the Latin for *worm*, which is *vermis*. The word appeared in Italian in the mid-1600s and literally means "little worms."
wimp	Etymologists believe that this word, used as an insult, came from *whimper*. *Wimp* entered our language in 1920.
wishy-washy	*Wishy-washy*, which means *indecisive*, has been in English since the late 1600s. It is a type of word formation based on *washy* (thin and watery).
X-ray	German scientist Wilhelm Röntgen (1845–1923) discovered and named *X-rays*. The *X* in the word stands for the unknown quantity *x*, and the *ray* is an English translation of the old German word *Strahlen* (rays, beams).
xylophone	The name for this musical instrument comes from the Greek *xýlon* (wood) and *phone* (English for "sound"). The word entered English in 1866, although similar African instruments can be traced to a much earlier time.
yam	This vegetable's name comes from the African *nyami* (eat). It originated with the Fulani ethnic group

found in northern Nigeria, Niger, and adjacent areas. As a food staple, huge yams, stacked like cordwood, are sold along the roads.

yolk
Yolk, in various spellings, has been in English since the 1300s. It came from an Old English (before 1100) word meaning "the yellow part," which is exactly what a yolk is.

zinger
Zinger is an American word made from *zing* (a fast, high-pitched sound or the addition of excitement to something) + *er*. A *zinger* can mean a clever, well-timed remark or a somewhat surprising turn of events.

zoo
Zoo is a clipping of *zoological gardens*. The word originally referred to the Zoological Gardens in Regents Park in London, established in the early 1800s. Some animal lovers think of a zoo as a confining place. For that reason, the words *wildlife conservation program with some permanent facilities* are sometimes used as a substitute. *Zoo* also can mean a noisy, chaotic place (e.g., When that store has a sale, the place is a *zoo*). This meaning has been around since before 1930.

Instructional Activity 2.1

Find the stories behind the following words. The works listed in the aforementioned endnote will be useful in locating their histories.

1. *backlog*
2. *coconut*
3. *eavesdrop*
4. *khaki*

5. *loophole*
6. *quarantine*
7. *turnpike*
8. *windfall*

"Borrowed" Words

Can you match the "borrowed" word with its country of origin (assuming present-day national boundaries)?

1. *boondocks*	A. Iceland
2. *cookie*	B. Armenia
3. *galore*	C. India
4. *geyser*	D. Tahiti
5. *guru*	E. Mexico
6. *jaguar*	F. Philippines
7. *shish kebab*	G. South Africa
8. *tatoo*	H. Netherlands
9. *tomato*	I. Paraguay
10. *trek*	K. Ireland

The correct answers are: *boondocks,* F. (Philippines); *cookie,* H. (Netherlands); *galore,* K. (Ireland); *geyser,* A. (Iceland); *guru,* C. (India); *jaguar,* I. (Paraguay); *shish kebab,* B. (Armenia); *tattoo,* D. (Tahiti); *tomato,* E. (Mexico); *trek,* G. (South Africa).[13]

The English language is composed of words from more than 120 languages.[14] And, as noted in *Wordworks,* some languages "borrow" words from one another because

a multicultural mix of people within a country ensures that words from other lands frequently will be used and will be absorbed by the most commonly used language. Another reason for borrowing is that sometimes there simply isn't an equivalent word in one's own language to describe a particular food, tree, computer part, ceremony, or the like.[15]

Bear in mind, however, that the term *borrowed words* is a misnomer because once we use the words, we do not give them back.[16]

From which countries did the words *broccoli, chipmunk,* and *philosophy* originate? A large dictionary will be helpful in your research.

2.2

Origins of Common Sayings

Just as every word has a story, familiar expressions do, too. Below are several common sayings and the stories behind them. Many of the sayings are idioms, which are discussed in Chapter 6.

> A *loose cannon* is someone who is out of control. The expression refers to sailors who feared that their heavy cannons would come loose from their restraints and endanger those on board and the ship itself.
>
> To *turn over a new leaf* means to begin anew. The expression can be traced to the early 1500s. The *leaf* in the expression isn't a plant leaf. It refers to a page in a book—presumably a book on how to behave properly.
>
> If a person is *under the weather,* that person is ill. Some scholars believe that the phrase reflects the weather's impact on health. Others think that the phrase comes from *under the weather bow*, which refers to the portion of a ship's bow that takes a beating in rough seas.
>
> When you pass a test *with flying colors,* you do so well that you'll probably get an A. The saying goes back to the 1600s, when ships that were victorious in battle returned home with their flags—that is, *colors*—flying.
>
> To *break the ice* comes from the world of commerce. In freezing weather, small ships were used to break up ice in waterways so that larger ships could pass. These small ships were known as *icebreakers*.

Today the expression means to make people comfortable in a somewhat tense or awkward situation.

When a person *pulls up stakes,* he or she moves to a new location. This American expression originated in colonial Boston and referred to the fact that when a family wanted to move, they literally pulled up the stakes that marked the boundary of their land.

To go scot-free dates back to the Middle Ages. In the 1300s a *scot* was a tax, so if one got off scot-free, that person did not have to pay a particular tax.

The expression *to fly the coop* has nothing to do with chickens. In the 1800s, *coop* was an American slang term for *jail,* so the saying meant to escape from being behind bars.

Since the early 1900s, a person who is overly formal in certain situations is referred to as a *stuffed shirt.* This expression comes from the motionless scarecrow whose shirt is filled with straw or paper.

When the New Jersey Turnpike was completed in 1951, it provided a left lane for drivers who wanted to travel faster. This *fast lane* is the basis for the saying *life in the fast lane.* The expression now means a somewhat reckless way of living.

To grab the brass ring refers to the practice whereby someone tries to pull a ring out of a box while riding on a carousel. If successful, that person would get a small prize. Today the expression means to reach for and achieve monetary success.

To pull out all the stops, meaning "to hold nothing back to achieve something," comes from the process of pulling out all of the knobs on an organ so that no pipe—and thus no sound—is silenced.

The walls have ears is a warning to speak cautiously because someone might be listening. The saying, from the early 1600s, originally had a literal meaning. In some European palaces, cuts discreetly were made in walls between rooms so that royalty could listen in on conversations.

To wing it means to be unprepared to do something but to do it anyway. The saying came from the theater. Actors who did not know their lines would get prompts from people in the wings of the stage.

To ham it up means to overact or exaggerate. This saying, too, comes from the theatrical world. *Ham* referred to the ham fat that actors used to remove stage makeup. The expression is American in origin and has been in use since the late 1930s.

To go haywire means to not function properly. The saying comes from difficulties in handling the wire that farmers used to "bale" or fasten bundles of hay together. The haywire became easily tangled.

Something that is *run-of-the-mill* is something that is common or routine. The expression is from the late 1800s. It referred to fabric from mills prior to its being sorted for quality.

To get the upper hand, which means to gain control of a situation, is an expression from a game that dates from the 1400s. One player put a hand at the bottom of a long stick, another player put a hand just above the previous player's hand, and this continued until the last person to get a hand at the top of a stick won the game.

The familiar expression *the three Rs* has been used since the early 1800s. It came from a former unschooled mayor of London who spoke about *reading, riting, and rithmetic.*[17]

Instructional Activity 2.3

Many familiar expressions are based on animals, insects, and fish. *Dog days of summer*, for example, comes from the ancient Romans, who believed that the hot, humid days of summer were influenced by the rising of the Dog Star, Sirius, with the sun. Complete the expressions below, using the clues in parentheses. Also try to locate the origins of at least two of the expressions. Answers are at the end of the chapter.

1. _____ business (foolishness)
2. take the _____ by the horns (take charge of a situation)
3. a loan _____ (one who charges a lot of interest on borrowed money)
4. to have _____ in your stomach (to be nervous)

5. a lounge _____ (one who is social and not too ambitious)
6. a legal _____ (a competent lawyer)
7. a one-_____ town (a small, dull village)
8. a _____ in sheep's clothing (someone who pretends to be good but is up to no good)
9. the straw that broke the _____ back (the final incident that makes someone lose patience)
10. a paper _____ (someone who appears powerful but actually is not)
11. cash _____ (something profitable that helps keep other ventures afloat)
12. _____ song (a final action)
13. as the _____ flies (in a straight line)
14. stir up a _____ nest (engage in something that will cause difficulties)
15. to smell a _____ (to be suspicious of someone or something)
16. wild-_____ chase (a worthless pursuit)
17. _____ feed (a small sum of money)
18. _____ food (green vegetables)
19. a sitting _____ (someone in a vulnerable position)
20. to _____ away (to put something aside for difficult times)

2.3

Answers to Instructional Activity 2.3

1. monkey	8. wolf	15. rat
2. bull	9. camel's	16. goose
3. shark	10. tiger	17. chicken
4. butterflies	11. cow	18. rabbit
5. lizard	12. swan	19. duck
6. eagle	13. crow	20. squirrel
7. horse	14. hornet's	

Notes

1. Robert K. Barnhart, ed., *The Barnhart Concise Dictionary of Etymology* (New York: HarperCollins, 1995).

2. Ibid., p. 369.

3. Editors of *Why Do We Say It? The Stories Behind the Words, Expressions and Clichés We Use* (Edison, NJ: Castle Books, 1985); Webb Garrison, *Why You Say It* (Nashville, TN: Rutledge Hill Press, 1992).

4. Barnhart, *The Barnhart Concise Dictionary of Etymology*, p. 332.

5. Editors, the *American Heritage®* Dictionaries, *More Word Histories and Mysteries from Aardvark to Zombie* (Boston: Houghton Mifflin, 2006); Laura Lee, *The Name's Familiar* (Gretna, LA: Pelican Publishing Company, 1999); Charles Panati, *Panati's Extraordinary Origins of Everyday Things* (New York: Harper & Row, 1987).

6. Craig M. Carver, *A History of English in Its Own Words* (New York: HarperCollins, 1991); Panati, *Panati's Extraordinary Origins of Everyday Things.*

7. Paul Dickson, *What's in a Name?* (Springfield, MA: Merriam-Webster, 1996).

8. Jonathan Evan Lighter, *Random House Historical Dictionary of American Slang*, vol. 2 (New York: Random House, 1997).

9. Tom McArthur, *The Concise Oxford Companion to the English Language* (Oxford, UK: Oxford University Press, 1996), p. 1032.

10. C. T. Onions, ed., *The Oxford Dictionary of English Etymology* (Oxford, UK: Oxford University Press, 1966).

11. Bonnie Johnson, *Wordworks: Exploring Language Play* (Golden, CO: Fulcrum Publishing, 1999).

12. John Ayto, *Dictionary of Word Origins* (New York: Arcade Publishing, 1990); John Ayto, *A Century of New Words* (Oxford, UK: Oxford University Press, 1999 [reprinted in 2006 and 2007]); Martha Barnette, *Ladyfingers & Nun's Tummies: A Lighthearted Look at How Foods Got Their Names* (New York: Times Books, 1997); Barnhart, *The Barnhart Concise Dictionary of Etymology*; David K. Barnhart and Allan A. Metcalf, *America in So Many Words: Words That Have Shaped America* (Boston: Houghton Mifflin, 1997); Lesley Brown, ed., *The New Shorter Oxford English Dictionary*, vols. 1 and 2 (Oxford, UK: Oxford University Press, 1973 [reprinted in 1993]); regarding the word *astronaut*: Paul Dickson, *Timelines* (New York: Addison-Wesley, 1990 [reprinted in 1991]); Editors of the *American Heritage®* Dictionaries, *Word Histories and Mysteries from Abracadabra to Zeus* (Boston: Houghton Mifflin, 2004); Editors of the *American Heritage®* Dictionaries *Word Histories and Mysteries from Aardvark to Zombie*; Editors, *Why Do We Say It?*; Morton S. Freeman, *The Story Behind the Word* (Philadelphia: Institute for Scientific Information Press, 1985); Charles Earle Funk, *A Hog on Ice & Other Curious Expressions* (New York: Harper & Row, 1948); Wilfred Funk, *Word Origins: An Exploration and History of Words and Language* (New York: Wings Books, 1950); Garrison, *Why You Say It*; Peter D. Jeans, *An Ocean of Words: A Dictionary of Nautical Words and Phrases* (Secaucus, NJ: Carol Publishing Group, 1993); Elizabeth Knowles, ed., *The Oxford Dictionary of New Words* (Oxford, UK: Oxford University Press, 1997); Lighter, *Random House Historical*

Dictionary of American Slang, vols. 1 and 2; regarding the phrase *wildlife conservation program with some permanent facilities:* William Lutz, *Doublespeak Defined* (New York: HarperCollins, 1999; Allan A. Metcalf, *The World in So Many Words* (Boston: Houghton Mifflin, 1999); Allan A. Metcalf, *Predicting New Words: The Secrets of Their Success* (Boston: Houghton Mifflin, 2002); William Morris and Mary Morris, *Morris Dictionary of Word and Phrase Origins,* 2nd ed. (New York: HarperCollins, 1977 [reprinted in 1988]); Onions, *The Oxford Dictionary of English Etymology*; Anne H. Soukhanov and Kathy Rooney, eds., *Encarta World English Dictionary* (New York: St. Martin's Press, 1999).

13. Brown, *The New Shorter Oxford English Dictionary,* vols. 1 and 2; Johnson, *Wordworks*; Metcalf, *The World in So Many Words*; Soukhanov and Rooney, *Encarta World English Dictionary.*

14. David Crystal, *The Cambridge Encyclopedia of the English Language* (Cambridge, UK: Cambridge University Press, 1995), p. 126.

15. Johnson, *Wordworks,* p. 172.

16. Ibid.

17. Christine Ammer, *The American Heritage® Dictionary of Idioms* (Boston: Houghton Mifflin, 1999); Funk, *A Hog on Ice & Other Curious Expressions*; Charles Earle Funk, *Heavens to Betsy! & Other Curious Sayings* (New York: Harper & Row [reprinted in 1983]); Webb Garrison, *Why You Say It*; Olivia A. Isil, *When a Loose Cannon Flogs a Dead Horse There's the Devil to Pay: Seafaring Words in Everyday Speech* (Camden, ME: International Marine, 1996); Laurence Urdang, Walter W. Hunsinger, and Nancy LaRoche, *A Fine Kettle of Fish and Other Figurative Phrases* (Detroit, MI: Visible Ink, 1991).

3

Word Formations

What do the phrases below have in common? Have you ever used any of them in your speaking or writing?

buddy-buddy	*flip-flop*
hush-hush	*fuddy-duddy*
goody-goody	*local-yokel*
no-no	*lovey-dovey*
yum-yum	*palsy-walsy*
rah-rah	*roly-poly*
ha-ha	*itty-bitty*
so-so	*pitter-patter*
dilly-dally	*teeny-weeny*
fender-bender	*wishy-washy*

These phrases are called *reduplicatives* because they are composed of words that are repeated verbatim or nearly so. Reduplicatives are one way that words are formed. In the previous chapter, we explored the diversity in the origins of words and noted that many English words have been taken from other languages. In this chapter, we look at how words are formed in English. As explained by British linguist Jean Aitchison, "Most words are not new at all, they are simply additions to existing words or recombinations of their elements. Words which are invented out of nothing are extremely rare."[1] The present chapter's focus is on *morphemes*, the building blocks in the formation of words. There are three broad ways in which words are formed in English: *word combining, word conversions and derivations,* and *word shortening.*

Word Combining

The formation of words through combining follows one of four paths. On the first path are *compound words* in which two words are joined to form a new word (e.g., *stop + light* = the compound *stoplight*). On the second path are *blended words* in which parts of two words are fused to form the new blended word (e.g., *information + commercial* = the blend *infomercial*). The third path involves the formation of contractions in which a word is combined with another word that has missing letters replaced by an apostrophe (e.g., *is + not* = the contraction *isn't*). On the fourth path is *reduplication*, which creates pairs of words that are identical or nearly identical as in the words at the beginning of this chapter (e.g., *hush-hush, pitter-patter*).

Compound Words

As stated above, compound words are formed by joining two words into one word. Some compound words retain elements of the meanings of the two words. Examples include *sunlight, flagpole, flying fish,* and *bridgebuilder.* George Miller calls this type of compound word *endocentric*; their meanings are named by the final word in the compound (e.g., light from the sun, a pole for flags, a fish that "flies," and a builder of bridges).[2] Other compound words refer to something other than what their parts refer to. Examples include *about-face* and *butterfly*. *About-face* is not a *face*, and a *butterfly* is not a *fly*. George Miller calls this type of compound *exocentric*. A co-author of the present book refers to them as *compound look-alikes*, and Tom McArthur calls them *holisms*.[3]

As you probably have noticed, compound words are written in three different ways. Some are single words (e.g., *cupcake*), some are two separate words (e.g., *patrol car*), and other compounds are hyphenated (e.g., *quick-freeze*). Sometimes compound words, particularly compounds with two words that are not joined together, are confused with noun phrases. For example, *gentleman* is a compound word but *gentle man* is a noun phrase. The word *very* can be used to determine if a word is a compound. A *very gentle man* makes sense, but a *very gentleman* does not because the latter is a compound word.

Many compound words originated in the United States long ago. H. L. Mencken reported the years during which the following compound words were coined:[4]

chewing gum (1850)
sweatshop (1867)
storm door (1878)
handout (1882)
monkey business (1883)
skyscraper (1883)
strikeout (1887)
shake-up (1887)
road hog (1893)
rubberneck (1900)
shut-in (1904)
highbrow (1905)
joyride (1909)
loan shark (1913)
jaywalker (1917)
trouble shooter (1931)

Some compounds (e.g., *road hog*) originated as slang, or what we call "in-betweens," but they have had staying power. That has not always been the case with compound words. Some fade from use quickly. Sol Steinmetz and Barbara Ann Kipfer note that the compound words *cushioncraft, dataphone, granny dress,* and *jet-hop* from the 1960s have become nearly extinct. And Tom McArthur has identified some compound words from the 1980s that have fallen from use: *blimp patrol, energy vampire,* and *punctuality nut.*[5]

Compound words differ in their underlying structures: *Whalebone* is the bone *of* a whale, *dining room* is a room *for* dining, and *rapid transit* is transit that *is* rapid. The following underlying structures for compound words have been identified.[6] These structures pertain to endocentric compounds (e.g., *carsick*) but not to exocentric compounds (e.g., *playoffs*). In each structure, *A* refers to the first word of the compound, and *B* refers to the second word of the compound.

B is in *A.*	A *shower drain* is a *drain* in the *shower.*
B is of *A.*	A *tuba player* is a *player* of *tubas.*
B is *A.*	*Barefoot* is a *foot* that is *bare.*
B is from *A.*	*Sunlight* is *light* from the *sun.*
B does *A.*	A *sailboat* is a *boat* that does *sail.*
B is for *A.*	A *flagpole* is a *pole* for *flags.*

Instructional Activity   3.1

Each of the following items contains synonyms or related words for two words. The two words, when combined, form a compound. (Example: *house* + *ill* = _____. The correct answer is *homesick.*) What are these compound words? Answers are at the end of the chapter.

1. *molar* + *pain* = _____
2. *mind* (noun) + *tornado* = _____
3. *correct* (verb) + *partner* = _____

4. *mug* + *torte* = _____
5. *pooch* + *lumber* (noun) = _____
6. *under* + *steps* (noun) = _____
7. *prepare food* + *novel* (noun) = _____
8. *orchestra* + *cart* (noun) = _____
9. *auto* + *harbor* (noun) = _____
10. *steer* (noun) + *young man* = _____

Now create your own puzzles with the following compound words: *armchair, billboard, cornstalk, greyhound, roadside, schoolhouse,* and *soundtrack.*

3.1

Blended Words

Blended words are formed by combining parts of two words (e.g., *guess* and *estimate = guesstimate, television* and *broadcast = telecast*). They differ from compound words, which join two whole words—not word parts. Blended words have been called *hybrids, fusions,* and *portmanteau* (port-mahn-TOE) words. Blends can be traced to the fifteenth and sixteenth centuries. Examples include *chortle* from *chuckle* and *snort* as well as *dumbfound* from *dumb* and *confound*. Many blends are American-made words formed in the last two centuries. Some blends traced by H. L. Mencken are *cablegram* (1868) from *cable* + *telegram, electrocute* (1880s) from *electricity* + *execute,* and *smog* (1905) from *smoke* + *fog.*[7]

Blends have been created to identify geographical areas. Examples include *Arklatex,* which refers to the intersection of Arkansas, Louisiana, and Texas; *Calexico,* which names the area where California and Mexico share a border; *Wisconsota* (Wisconsin and Minnesota boundary); and *Eurasia* (Europe and Asia). Some blends are formed from corporate names (*Sunoco* for Sun Oil Company), language fusions (*Spanglish* for Spanish and English), product names (*Breathalyzer* for Breath analyzer), culinary creations (*Spamwich* for Spam® sandwich), geographical features (*Chunnel* for the English Channel plus tunnel), hybrid animals (*beefalo* for beef cattle plus buffalo), and new ideas or labels (*politoons* for political cartoons). Additional blends in common use include:

Amtrak	American—track
avionics	aviation—electronics
bit	binary—digit
blotch	blot—botch
blurt	blare—spurt
broasted	broiled—roasted
caplet	capsule—tablet
clump	chunk—lump
flare	flame—glare
flurry	flutter—hurry
glimmer	gleam—shimmer
heliport	helicopter—airport
Medicaid	Medical—aid
Medicare	Medical—care
meld	melt—weld
moped	motor—pedal
motorcade	motor—cavalcade
paratrooper	parachute—trooper
pixel	picture—elements
quasar	quasi—stellar
scuzzy	scummy—fuzzy
simulcast	simultaneous—telecast
slanguage	slang—language
slosh	slop—slush
smash	smack—mash
splatter	splash—spatter
squiggle	squirm—wriggle
telethon	television—marathon
travelogue	travel—monologue
twirl	twist—whirl

Tom McArthur points out that the formation of blends appears to be on the increase, particularly in corporate and product development use. Their number at present is unclear, but in the 1977 edition of *The American Language*, H. L. Mencken cited a doctoral dissertation that lists 3,500 distinct word blends—and that was more than thirty years ago.[8]

Contractions

Contractions are words that are formed by fusing a whole word with another word that has a deleted letter or letters replaced with an apostrophe (e.g., *I'd—I would, you've—you have*). Contractions have been in use at least since the time of Shakespeare, and they occur frequently in conversational English and informal speech and writing. There are no rules that govern when one should or should not use a contraction. The most common contractions include negatives such as *don't* and *isn't* and auxiliary verb contractions for the following: *is* (e.g., *it's*), *am* (e.g., *I'm*), *are* (e.g., *we're*), *will* (e.g., *they'll*), *have* (e.g., *you've*), *had* (e.g., *we'd*), and *would* (e.g., *she'd*).

Some linguists think of contractions as shortened words, but as we will see, they are not at all similar to abbreviations or clippings. We list them in the category of word combining because they join words and parts of words.

Reduplicatives

Reduplication involves doubling a word or word element and its sound for purposes of emphasis. Reduplicatives can be found in many languages and occur with some frequency in English. In several reduplicatives, the words are repeated (e.g., *hush-hush*) and hyphenated. Tom McArthur calls these words *echoic* reduplicatives.[9] More frequently, reduplicatives contain identical elements and contrasting elements (e.g., *lovey-dovey*). As long ago as 1870, Ebenezer Cobham Brewer called such reduplicatives *ricochet* words.[10] Here are two lists of reduplicatives. Meanings are given for those that are not commonly used.

Echoic Reduplicative	Ricochet Reduplicative
no-no	*sing-song* (rising and falling pitch)
tsk-tsk (shame on someone)	*riff-raff* (ill-mannered people)
bye-bye	*dilly-dally* (waste time)
choo-choo	*hoity-toity* (snobbish)
ha-ha	*flim-flam* (swindle)
goody-goody (almost too nice)	*hodge-podge* (a mixture)
pooh-pooh (disregard)	*pee-wee* (tiny)
buddy-buddy (overly friendly)	*rag tag* (messy, unkempt)
lulu (a big mistake)	*rinky-dink* (foolish, unimportant)
rah-rah	*willy-nilly* (haphazard)

Instructional Activity 3.2

Can you solve these riddles? In each case, the answer will be an echoic or a ricochet reduplicative. Answers are at the end of the chapter.

1. What is another word for *mediocre*?
2. What does a time-waster do?
3. What do people who change their positions on something do?
4. What is a person called who won't take a stand?
5. What do we say when we like the taste of something?
6. What do you do when you walk a crooked path?
7. What is the sound of gentle rain on a roof?
8. What is a car accident that is not serious?
9. What do you call something that is exceptional?
10. What do you call someone who has lived in the same place for a long time?

3.2

As demonstrated in the section above, words in English have been formed through four types of word combining: compounding, blending, contracting, and reduplicating. In the next section, we examine the formation of new words through conversion and derivation.

Word Conversions and Derivations

Conversions change a word from one part of speech to another without changing the form of the word (e.g., changing *paper* from a noun as in *a piece of paper* to a verb as in *to paper a room*). The most common type of conversion, changing a noun to a verb, is shown in the sentence "We *oil* the pedals and then *bicycle* to the park to *sandwich in* a quick picnic."[11] As Tom McArthur notes, "It is often said that 'there is no noun in English that can't be verbed': *bag* a prize, *doctor* a drink, *position* a picture."[12] Conversions accomplish the change of a word from one part of speech to another without the addition of any affixes (i.e., prefixes or suffixes). In addition to the noun-to-verb conversions, there are others that commonly occur:

verb to noun	One who *cheats* on a test will be known as a *cheat*.
noun to adjective	My I.D. card is made of *plastic*. *Plastic* cards are more durable.
adjective to noun	How was the *final* exam? Did you pass the *final*?
adjective to verb	We don't have a *dry* towel, but we still have to *dry* the dishes.

Derivations are words that are formed from less complex words through the addition of prefixes or suffixes (e.g., the verb *enjoy* is changed to the noun *enjoyment* through the addition of the suffix *-ment*). Linguists differentiate *inflections* from *derivations*, although both involve the addition of suffixes. *Inflections* are suffixes that do not change the syntax—the grammatical part of speech of the root word. They affect only verb tense (e.g., *walk, walks, walking*), plurality (e.g., *party, parties*), comparison (e.g., *small, smaller, smallest*), and possession (e.g., *children's, dogs'*). Derivational suffixes create a new word out of an old word by changing the syntactic function of the word (e.g., *believe* is a verb, *believable* is an adjective).

Steven Pinker has identified the following twenty-eight suffixes as the most common in English:[13]

-a	*-ism*
-ate	*-ness*
-ify	*-ance*
-ize	*-ful*
-able	*-ist*
-ed	*-ory*
-ion	*-ant*
-ly	*-hood*
-age	*-ity*
-en	*-ous*
-ish	*-ary*
-ment	*-ic*
-an	*-ive*
-er	*-y*

Some suffixes signal words as nouns. For example:

-ance	*tolerate—tolerance*
-ation	*starve—starvation*
-age	*spill—spillage*
-ant	*inform—informant*
-dom	*wise—wisdom*
-eer	*auction—auctioneer*
-er	*buy—buyer*
-ery	*drudge—drudgery*
-hood	*state—statehood*
-ier	*finance—financier*
-ing	*surf—surfing*
-ion, -tion	*exhibit—exhibition*
-ism	*true—truism*

-ist	*elite—elitist*
-ity	*inferior—inferiority*
-ment	*govern—government*
-ness	*awkward—awkwardness*
-ty	*honest—honesty*

Some suffixes signal words as adjectives. For example:

-able	*change—changeable*
-al	*function—functional*
-en	*gold—golden*
-ful	*help—helpful*
-ish	*pig—piggish*
-ive	*protect—protective*
-like	*ape—apelike*
-ous	*humor—humorous*
-wards	*back—backwards*
-wise	*clock—clockwise*

Two common suffixes that signal verbs are *-ify* (e.g., *beauty—beautify*) and *-ize* (e.g., *personal—personalize*).

Some suffixes emanated from slang and became popular for a time before gradually fading from use. The suffix *-ville* is an example. In the 1950s, frequently used *-ville* words included *dullsville, ho-humsville, yawnsville, weirdsville, yucksville, lootsville, slicksville,* and dozens of others not heard much since the 1960s. The suffix *-o* (e.g., *daddy-o*), which has been traced to the 1920s, reemerged in the 1950s in words such as *weirdo, sicko, creepo, whacko, righto, wrongo.*[14] The suffix *-y* has been in use since its emerging popularity in the 1960s as in *scuzzy, grubby, pricey, draggy,* and *yucky.* The suffix *-gate* came into wide use in the 1970s from the Washington complex Watergate, site of a burglary in the Democratic Party headquarters. The burglary prompted the undoing of President Richard Nixon and caused his resignation in

1974. Since that time, *-gate* has been attached to scandalous activities, real or imagined, including *Fajitagate, Katrinagate, Nannygate, Travelgate,* and *Troopergate,* which was used during the 2008 presidential campaign.

Prefixes also are used to form derivations, although in English, prefixes are fewer in number than suffixes. Some prefixes have more than one meaning (e.g., *un-* can mean *not* in *unable* or a reverse action in *unwrap*). Some meanings have more than one prefix. For example, the meaning *not* is represented in the words *un*willing, *il*legible, *ir*rational, *dis*loyal, *in*active, *im*polite, *un*constitutional, and *non*combustible. Common invariant prefixes—those with only one meaning—include:

Prefix	Invariant Meaning	Sample Word
circum-	around	circumnavigate
e-	electronic	e-book
equi-	equal	equidistant
extra-	outside	extracurricular
I-	Internet	I-tools
intra-	within	intraoffice
mal-	not	maladjusted
mis-	not	misunderstood
non-	not	nonprofit
syn-	same	synonym

Prefixes affect the root words that they adjoin in five major ways:

number	*mono*syllable, *bi*focal, *semi*annual, *tri*angle
size or degree	*arch*enemy, *mini*market, *mega*store, *ultra*light
time or order	*ex*-husband, *pre*test, *post*test, *re*enlist
negation	*dis*agree, *in*accurate, *un*stated, *dys*functional
reversal	*un*tie, *de*ice, *dis*assemble

Instructional Activity 3.3

Which prefix would best fit the root words in each group? Possible answers are at the end of the chapter.

Group One	Group Two	Group Three
_____do	_____taste	_____social
_____write	_____ward	_____intellectual
_____organize	_____thought	_____war

Group Four	Group Five	Group Six
_____descript	_____possible	_____due
_____conformist	_____mature	_____do
_____partisan	_____polite	_____bearing

3.3

Instructional Activity 3.4

Which suffix would best fit the root words in each group? Possible answers are at the end of the chapter.

Group One	Group Two	Group Three
arrange _____	ash_____	thought_____
settle_____	wood_____	joy_____
endear_____	earth_____	fear_____

Group Four	Group Five	Group Six
kind_____	free_____	paint_____
dark_____	bore_____	work_____
good_____	martyr_____	teach_____

3.4

Word Shortening

There are two ways in which words are formed through the shortening of other words: *abbreviations* and *clippings*. Abbreviations usually retain the initial letters of the words being shortened as in *APA* for American Psychological Association. Clipped words retain a part of the word but not all of it as in *condo* clipped from *condominium*.

Abbreviations

Abbreviations fall into three categories. *Acronyms* are abbreviations that can be pronounced as words; for example, *PIN* stands for Personal Identification Number and *FEMA* stands for Federal Emergency Management Agency. *Initialisms* must be spoken as a sequence of letters as in *ATM* for Automatic Teller Machine and *FBI* for Federal Bureau of Investigation. Initialisms are not pronounced as words. The third type of abbreviation is the FWO, which means For Writing Only.[15] Examples include *Blvd.* for Boulevard and *Dr.* for Doctor. FWOs are similar to clippings but appear only in written English because they are often difficult to pronounce as acronyms and are not spoken as individual letters.

Examples of each of the three types of abbreviations are given below.

Acronyms

AMEX	American Express
ARM	Adjustable Rate Mortgage
Epcot®	Experimental Prototype Community of Tomorrow
FICA	Federal Insurance Contributions Act
EURAIL	European Railway
NASCAR	National Association for Stock Car Auto Racing
NATO	North Atlantic Treaty Organization
OPEC	Organization of Petroleum Exporting Countries
OSHA	Occupational Safety and Health Administration
VISTA	Volunteers in Service to America

Initialisms

ATV	All Terrain Vehicle
COD	Cash on Delivery
CPR	Cardio-Pulmonary Resuscitation
EPA	Environmental Protection Agency
ER	Emergency Room
GNP	Gross National Product
GPA	Grade Point Average
NPR	National Public Radio
TBA	To Be Announced

FWOs

acct.	account
adj.	adjective
amt.	amount
attn.	attention
bldg.	building
encl.	enclosure
etc.	et cetera
govt.	government
mfg.	manufacturing
misc.	miscellaneous
qt.	quart
tbsp.	tablespoon
dept.	department
co.	company

Acronyms have been around for many years, but their numbers surged during World War II when the military used them as a form of short-hand. Acronyms such as *WAC* (Women's Army Corps), *RADAR* (Radio Detection and Ranging), and *UNICEF* (United Nations International Children's Emergency Fund) came into use during that period.

The administration of President Franklin Delano Roosevelt (who often is referred to by the initialism *FDR*) brought America out of the Great Depression through his legislation known as the New Deal. This legislation spawned the initialisms *PWA* (Public Works Administration), *WPA* (Works Progress Administration), *CCC* (Civilian Conservation Corps), *TVA* (Tennessee Valley Authority), *FSA* (Farm Security Administration), *NRA* (National Recovery Administration), and others. Initialisms were so prevalent during FDR's years in office that his programs were referred to as "alphabet soup."[16]

Instructional Activity 3.5

Every airport has an identification code that is either an acronym or an initialism. Although the abbreviation may seem odd for some airports, there is an explanation for each code. The source for some codes, such as DFW for Dallas–Fort Worth, is clear. ORD for Chicago's O'Hare Airport is not so obvious. The abbreviation comes from *Orchard Field*, which is what the area was called in 1946. The airport was renamed *O'Hare* in 1949 in honor of World War II navy pilot Edward O'Hare, who died in combat at age 29.[17]

Match the following cities with their correct airport code. The answers are at the end of the chapter.

1.	Baltimore, Maryland	LAX
2.	Canton/Akron, Ohio	HOT
3.	Los Angeles, California	AZO
4.	Fresno, California	LCH
5.	Green Bay, Wisconsin	BWI
6.	Hot Springs, Arkansas	ALO
7.	Kalamazoo, Michigan	TPA
8.	Lake Charles, Louisiana	CAK
9.	Waterloo, Iowa	GRB
10.	Tampa, Florida	FAT

How widespread is the use of abbreviations in English? Very. The 40th edition of *Acronyms, Initialisms, and Abbreviations Dictionary* lists 912,980 entries.[18] Many abbreviations refer to more than one entity. *IRA*, for example, can refer to Individual Retirement Account, International Reading Association, and Irish Republican Army—to name a few.

3.5

Clipped Words

Clipping is another type of word formation through shortening. Unlike acronyms and initialisms, which are usually built from the first letter of each word, *clipped words* are formed by deleting elements of the word (e.g., *lab* for *laboratory*, *plane* for *airplane*). Clipping is done in one of three ways: The back of the word is clipped as in *ump* for *umpire*, the front of the word is clipped as in *gator* for *alligator*, or elements are clipped from the front and the back of the word as in *flu* for *influenza*. Some clipped words undergo a change in spelling: *nuke* for *nuclear*, *trank* for *tranquilizer*, *perk* for *perquisite*, *fax* for *facsimile*, *bike* for *bicycle*, and *mike* for *microphone*. Clipped words remain identical in meaning to the original word. Examples of the three types of clipped words include:

Clipped Words—Back Removed
rhino—rhinoceros
super—superintendent
tux—tuxedo
champ—champion
demo—demonstration
ref—referee
vet—veteran, veterinarian
memo—memorandum
limo—limousine
legit—legitimate
chimp—chimpanzee
hippo—hippopotamus

mayo—mayonnaise
rehab—rehabilitation
typo—typographical
drape—drapery
con—convict
sub—submarine

Clipped Words—Front Removed
quake—earthquake
burbs—suburbs
hood—neighborhood
though—although
mum—chrysanthemum
van—caravan
burger—hamburger
fries—french fries
gator—alligator
tie—necktie

Words that have both their front and back clipped (e.g., *fridge* from *refrigerator* and *Liz* from *Elizabeth*) are few in number.

Several clipped words are related to education:

econ—economics
anthro—anthropology
math—mathematics
phys ed—physical education
trig—trigonometry
poli-sci—political science
el ed—elementary education
Western civ—Western civilization
soc—sociology
psych—psychology
alum—alumnus

grad—graduate
undergrad—undergraduate
prof—professor

Many individuals go by a clipped form of their first name: *Don, Dan, Marv, Pat, Jan, Stan, Ray, Barb, Steve, Pete, Jen, Zack,* and so on.

In the past, critics of clipped words considered them undignified and of low quality or not suitable for any kind of literary or serious writing. Nonetheless, the practice of clipping words has a long history in American English. H. L. Mencken dated some common clipped words: *photo* (1863), *bike* (1882), *phone* (1886), *co-ed* (1889), *auto* (1899), and *gas* (1905).[19]

Text messaging (*texting, txtng*) refers to the various shorthands in use in electronic communication based on point-to-point Short Message Service (SMS). These shorthands were first used experimentally in the early 1990s in Finland, achieved wide use in Japan, and then spread worldwide rapidly. In 2001, 12.2 billion text messages were sent in the United Kingdom alone among the 250 billion text messages sent internationally that year. More recently, American 13- to 17-year-olds have sent or received an average 1,742 text messages a month per user, and the numbers continue to grow. In 2006, 158 billion text messages were sent in the United States; that number now is in the trillions per year.[20]

The texting "language" comprises several of the word-shortening categories described in this chapter as well as other categories:

initialisms: *brb* = be right back, *cmb* = call me back, *fwiw* = for what it's worth, *idk* = I don't know, *ptmm* = please tell me more
words with omitted letters: *btr* = better, *cupl* = couple, *prt* = party, *w* = with, *wknd* = weekend
clipped words: *absol* = absolutely, *arr* = arrive, *diff* = different, *prob* = probably, *max* = maximum
nonstandard spellings: *cuz* = because, *skul* = school, *thanx* = thanks, *thru* = through, *wanna* = want to
words with symbols and numbers: *2* = to, *b4* = before, *2day* = today, *1dful* = wonderful, *l8r* = later.

There are a number of ways to explain the phenomenal popularity of text messaging. Those cited by Louis Menand and others include: Texting saves time and energy, because of speed it is cheaper than talking on mobile phones, it is a sign of prestige among some groups, it is immediate and personal, it is fun because it is a form of word play, and users with imagination can create new word shortenings.[21] Texting gives privacy where voice messages could be overheard, and it can be accomplished in a noisy environment. It also enables universities and corporations to alert students and employees to imminent dangers. A potential downside, however, is that text messaging promotes multitasking (e.g., texting while walking, driving, or sitting in class); some states want to enact laws that ban text messaging while driving and walking because of safety concerns.[22] Nevertheless, we predict that txting wl b arnd 4 a lng tim.

Answers to Instructional Activity 3.1

1. *toothache*
2. *brainstorm*
3. *checkmate*
4. *cupcake*
5. *dogwood*
6. *downstairs*
7. *cookbook*
8. *bandwagon*
9. *carport*
10. *cowboy*

Answers to Instructional Activity 3.2

1. *so-so*
2. *dilly-dally*
3. *flip-flop*
4. *wishy-washy*
5. *yum-yum*
6. *zig-zag*
7. *pitter-patter*

8. *fender-bender*
9. *super-duper*
10. *local-yokel*

Possible Answers to Instructional Activity 3.3

Group One	Group Two	Group Three
re-	*after-*	*anti-*
Group Four	**Group Five**	**Group Six**
non-	*im-*	*over-*

Possible Answers to Instructional Activity 3.4

Group One	Group Two	Group Three
-ment	*-en*	*-ful*
Group Four	**Group Five**	**Group Six**
-ness	*-dom*	*-er*

Answers to Instructional Activity 3.5

1.	Baltimore, Maryland	BWI
2.	Canton/Akron, Ohio	CAK
3.	Los Angeles, California	LAX
4.	Fresno, California	FAT
5.	Green Bay, Wisconsin	GBR
6.	Hot Springs, Arkansas	HOT
7.	Kalamazoo, Michigan	AZO
8.	Lake Charles, Louisiana	LCH
9.	Waterloo, Iowa	ALO
10.	Tampa, Florida	TPA

Notes

1. Jean Aitchison, *Words in the Mind: An Introduction to the Mental Lexicon*, 2nd ed. (Oxford, UK: Blackwell, 1994), p. 158.

2. George A. Miller, *The Science of Words* (New York: Scientific American Library, 1996).

3. Ibid.; Bonnie Johnson, *Wordworks: Exploring Language Play* (Golden, CO: Fulcrum Publishing, 1999); Tom McArthur, *The Concise Oxford Companion to the English Language* (Oxford, UK: Oxford University Press, 1996).

4. H. L. Mencken, *The American Language* (New York: Alfred A. Knopf, 1977), pp. 205–206.

5. Sol Steinmetz and Barbara Ann Kipfer, *The Life of Language* (New York: Random House, 2006), p. 195; McArthur, *The Concise Oxford Companion to the English Language*, p. 230.

6. Dale D. Johnson and P. David Pearson, *Teaching Reading Vocabulary*, 2nd ed. (Fort Worth, TX: Holt, Rinehart and Winston, 1984), pp. 132–133.

7. Mencken, *The American Language.*

8. McArthur, *The Concise Oxford Companion to the English Language.*

9. Ibid.

10. Cited in Steinmetz and Kipfer, *The Life of Language.*

11. Johnson, *Wordworks*, p. 150.

12. McArthur, *The Concise Oxford Companion to the English Language*, p. 242.

13. Steven Pinker, *The Language Instinct: How the Mind Creates Language* (New York: William Morrow, 1994), pp. 128–129.

14. Johnson, *Wordworks*, p. 149.

15. Ibid., pp. 165–166.

16. Library of Congress, Great Depression and World War II, 1929–1945: President Franklin Delano Roosevelt and the New Deal, 1933–1945, Library of Congress, 2008, http://lcweb2.loc.gov/learn/features/timeline/depwwii/newdeal/newdeal.html.

17. Airwise.com, 2008, Chicago O'Hare, http://www.airwise.com/airports/us/ORD/ORD_07.html.

18. Linda Hall, ed., *Acronyms, Initialisms, and Abbreviations Dictionary*, 40th ed. (Farmington Hills, MI: Gale Cengage, 2008).

19. Mencken, *The American Language*, p. 203.

20. David Crystal, *txtng: the gr8 db8* (Oxford, UK: Oxford University Press, 2008); Louis Menand, "Thumbspeak: Is Texting Here to Stay?" *New Yorker*, October 20, 2008; Jennifer Steinhauer and Laura M. Holson, "Cellular Alert: As Texts Fly, Danger Lurks," *New York Times*, September 20, 2008.

21. Menand, "Thumbspeak."

22. Steinhauer and Holson, "Cellular Alert."

4

Semantic Connections

How Words Are Organized in Our Minds

What connections do you make when you see or hear the word *stick*?

*a small tree branch, stick of gum, stick pin, stick shift, stick-tight, stick fig-
ure, stick around, stick to it, stick it to, stick together, a stick-up, stick up
for, stick by, sticky, stick-in-the-mud, stick your neck out, stick out like a
sore thumb, stick your nose into something, stick to your guns, a sticky situation, a sticker, stickies, a sticking point, a sticky wicket, sticker price,
sticker shock, stick to your ribs, a stickler, a stick of paratroopers, not a
stick of furniture, lives in the sticks, sticks and stones may break my bones
but words can never hurt me.*

Every time we speak or write, we select words from the gargantuan
storehouse of American English. When we listen or read, words trigger

our understanding. We seem to use words effortlessly, and we rarely give them a thought. *Words* have been defined as "graphic configurations bordered by space," "labels for concepts," "linguistic units of sound and print that represent meanings," and more. Detailed and elaborate definitions of *words* are found in large dictionaries and reference works.

Semantics is the meaning system of a language, comprising the words with all their denotations (what the words explicitly mean), connotations (shades of meanings), and ambiguities (unclear meanings). The focus of this chapter is the semantic or meaning system of English. Semanticists study the vocabulary of a language (i.e., the lexicon) in all its forms and senses. The lexicon of English is ever-changing through the creation of *neologisms,* or new words (e.g., *scratchiti*); the changing meanings of older words (e.g., *bully*); the addition of words from other languages (e.g., *quesadilla* from Mexican Spanish); and the abandonment of words that fall out of use and become virtually extinct (e.g., years ago, *kew-kaw* meant *upside-down*).[1]

How many words are there in English? The twenty-volume *Oxford English Dictionary* (http://www.oed.com), considered to be the most comprehensive in English, contains 291,500 different entry words (e.g., *run*), and 616,100 word forms (e.g., *ran, running*). The influential *Roget's International Thesaurus*[2] holds 330,000 different words and phrases, and the single-volume *Encarta World English Dictionary*[3] has more than 100,000 entry words. Estimates of the total size of the English lexicon range upward to more than 2 million *lexemes.*[4] Linguists, people who study language, use the terms *lexical item* or *lexeme* as a more inclusive term than *word* for a unit of meaning because *lexeme* encompasses idioms (e.g., *to have a green thumb*), abbreviations (e.g., *Dr.*), and logograms (e.g., *$, &*) as well as words. In this volume, *word* and *lexeme* are used interchangeably. One reason a precise count of the number of lexemes of English is not possible is that there are so many multiple-meaning words in our lexicon. Consider the word *rock* in the following sentences.

A geologist classified the *rock.*
Don't *rock* the boat.

That's some *rock* she has on her finger.

He will *rock* the baby to sleep.

The prison, Alcatraz, was called the *Rock*.

Do you like *rock* music?

I'm between a *rock* and a hard place.

She is the *rock* in that family.

This is my *rock*-bottom price.

These are nine different meanings of the word *rock*, so in determining a lexicon's size, should *rock* be counted as a single word or as nine words? Multiple-meaning words are so plentiful in English that we devote an entire chapter to them in this book.

One's personal vocabulary is called one's *mental lexicon*. What does it mean to "know" a word? Does it mean to know the word's definition or spelling or pronunciation or usage or synonyms or all of these things and more? The words in our mental lexicon are the words that we can understand and use to communicate. Learning the specific size of anyone's personal vocabulary is an imprecise undertaking; it can be accomplished only by estimation. Several linguists have approached the task and have either conducted or reviewed language acquisition research. Estimates of average mental-lexicon size range from 14,000 words for 6-year-olds[5] to 45,000 words for high school graduates,[6] and up to 200,000 words for college graduates.[7] Jean Aitchison and Eve V. Clark have examined the nature, organization, and acquisition of the mental lexicon, one's individual storehouse of known words.[8]

Semantic Categories

How is the immense lexicon of English organized in one's mind? Linguists examine sets of related words that share different aspects of core meanings. *Semantic categories* (called *semantic fields* by linguists) are the interconnected systems of words that relate in some way to a central concept. Semantic categories enable us to learn new words in ways that are made meaningful by the semantic relationships these words share with others in a given category. As demonstrated by the *stick* example at the beginning of this chapter, a single word can set off an explosion of connections among words in many categories.

One of the first and most influential attempts to identify the central concepts of the major semantic networks, along with the semantic categories and words related to them, was that of Peter Mark Roget (1779–1869). In 1852, he published the *Thesaurus of English Words and Phrases, Classified and Arranged so as to Facilitate the Expression of Ideas and Assist in Literary Composition.* Roget's scholarly attainments were numerous and included earning a medical degree at age 19, being elected a fellow of the Royal Academy, and contributing articles to the *Encyclopedia Britannica.* Roget envisioned his system of verbal classification in 1805 and began serious work on the thesaurus in 1849.[9] The distinction between a thesaurus as developed by Roget and a dictionary is an important one. Dictionaries are organized alphabetically, thereby giving readers speedy access to words of interest. But alphabetical order has no semantic reality. Words that are related to one another through shared semantic categories are kept apart in a dictionary but are grouped together in a thesaurus. A dictionary goes from word to meaning, but a thesaurus goes from meaning to word. A thesaurus generalizes and a dictionary particularizes. The organization of words in our mental lexicons is more similar to the structure of a thesaurus than to that of a dictionary.

Most people who know Roget's *Thesaurus* view it as a comprehensive indexed collection of synonyms that can be useful if one is searching for an alternative word or is in need of a word to label an idea. To create his thesaurus, Roget established six classes (called *semantic networks* or *unique beginners* by modern linguists): Abstract Relations, Space, Matter, Intellect, Volition, and Affections. By the sixth edition of *Roget's International Thesaurus,*[10] the number of classes had been expanded from Roget's original six to fourteen. They include: The Body and the Senses, Feelings, Place and Change of Place, Measure and Shape, Living Things, Natural Phenomenon, Behavior and the Will, Language, Human Society and Institutions, Values and Ideals, Arts, Occupations and Crafts, Sports and Amusements, and The Mind and Ideas. These fourteen semantic networks incorporate 1,075 semantic categories and 330,000 words and phrases. The *Random House Word Menu,* developed by Stephen Glazier,[11] is a comprehensive reference work consisting of 800 semantic categories and 75,000 entry words. It functions as a thesaurus, dictionary, and reverse dictionary, and it is a compilation of synonyms, antonyms, and related words organized by category.

In the fall of 2009, Oxford University Press published the *Historical Thesaurus of the Oxford English Dictionary.* This monumental thesaurus contains 920,000 words with 797,120 meanings organized into 354 major categories and 236,400 subcategories. The project took forty-four years to complete.[12]

Meaning Relations

Linguists use the terms *sense relations*[13] or *meaning relations*[14] to describe the systematic patterns found in the ways words relate to one another within semantic categories. *Doctor* and *patient* share a meaning relationship, but the words *saturate* and *window* do not. The meaning relations that explain how words relate to one another in our mental lexicons are the following: *synonymy, antonomy, hyponomy, meronomy, attribution, function,* and *polysemy,* as well as *collocations, series,* and *hierarchies.* All are described next.

Categories of Meaning Relations

synonymy: *Synonyms* are words with nearly identical or very similar meanings (e.g., *thrifty, frugal, cheap, penny-pincher*). Schoolchildren learn that synonyms are words that mean the same thing, but that is not literally true. Synonyms take on subtly different meanings in different contexts. A *thrifty* person might be considered wise, but a *penny-pincher* would be considered miserly.

antonomy: *Antonyms* are words with opposite meanings, but not all antonym pairs are opposite in quite the same way. In fact, there are three broad categories of antonyms: (a) *Gradable antonyms* are word pairs that exist on a continuum from one extreme to the other. Size can comprise one such continuum as in *gigantic, huge, large, medium, small, tiny, minuscule.* The pairs *gigantic—minuscule, huge—tiny,* and *large—small* are gradable antonyms. (b) *Complementary antonyms* are mutually exclusive word pairs. In each pair, one word negates the possibility of the other word. The entity being described cannot be both (e.g., *living—dead, open—closed, awake—asleep, in—out*). (c) *Converse antonyms* are word pairs in which one antonym in the pair implies that the other antonym needs to exist (e.g., *teacher—student, parent—child, buy—sell*).

Linguists use the term *hypernym* to mean superordinate word or, more simply, category label. In the category *Tools: saw, hammer, pliers, wrench,* for example, *Tools* is the hypernym, or category label, and the other words are members of the *Tools* category. The following four types of meaning relations show ways that different words in a category are related to the hypernym, the superordinate word.

hyponomy: *Hyponyms* are members or examples of the category named by the hypernym. Hyponyms of the hypernym *Dog* include *schnauzers, poodles, bulldogs,* and *collies.*

meronomy: *Meronyms* are words that signify parts of the hypernym. Meronyms of the hypernym *Dog* include *paws, tails, teeth,* and *coat.*

attribution: *Attributes* are semantic features that describe the hypernym. Attributes of *Dog* include *loyal, hungry,* and *protective.*

function: *Functions* are words that tell what the hypernym does or what is done to it. Functions of *Dog* include *barking, growling, fetching, guiding, rescuing,* and *grooming.*

The remaining categories of meaning relations are as follows:

polysemy: *Polysemous* words are multiple-meaning words, as exemplified earlier by the words *stick* and *rock.* These words are spelled the same but have different meanings and sometimes different pronunciations (e.g., *conduct*).

collocations: *Collocations* are pairs of words that frequently occur together in English. When we see one of the words in such pairs, we usually see the other word adjacent or nearby. Examples of collocations are *hermetically sealed, torrential downpour, unruly behavior.*

series: Some words relate to each other because of their placement in a *series.* Examples include numerical order (e.g., *one, two*), days of the week, and months of the year.

hierarchies: Words that occur in a hierarchical series hold rankings in relation to one another. The sizes of eggs comprise a hierarchy (e.g., *jumbo, extra-large, large, medium, small, peewee*). The same is true for military ranks (e.g., *general, colonel, major, captain*).

Semantic categories, in summary, are sets of words that share some relationship to a central concept and to one another. Semantic categories provide ways of "cutting up the lexicon [vocabulary] along semantic lines to group together lexical items [words] related to each other in a variety of ways."[15] Ten types of sense or meaning relationships, as listed above, are found among words in the semantic categories. Semantic categories may be divided into subcategories, and they are also parts of larger semantic networks.

The Mental Lexicon

One of the oldest measures designed to examine how words might be stored in our mental lexicons is the Word Association Test invented by Sir Francis Galton (1822–1911) and described by George Miller in *The Science of Words.*[16] The test requires subjects to provide the words or thoughts that immediately come to their minds when they hear a test word. According to Miller, the first large-scale study in English was conducted by G. H. Kent and A. J. Rosanoff in 1910.[17] One thousand subjects said the first word that came to mind for each of a hundred test words. The word *chair*, for example, evoked such responses as *table, seat, sit, furniture, wood, rocker, legs,* and others. Responses in a number of word association studies indicate that most of the associations that people make are of the following types:

> hypernyms—category label (e.g., *furniture* is a category that includes *chair*)
>
> hyponyms—members of a category (e.g., *table, desk, sofa,* and *chair* are members of the *furniture* category)
>
> attribute words (e.g., *wood, hickory,* and *plastic* can describe a *chair*)
>
> meronyms—parts of a whole (e.g., *seat, back, legs,* and *cushion* are parts of a *chair*)
>
> function words (e.g., *sit, rock*)
>
> synonyms (e.g., *stool, bench*)

In this context, George Miller asks and answers an intriguing question:

> The word association test demonstrates that a single word can make available, or activate, a wide range of lexical knowledge, [but] can the pooled data for a large group of people be taken as representative of the mental lexicon for any single individual? The answer is yes.[18]

Word association research findings have indeed demonstrated that words in our mental lexicons are organized by semantic categories and by the meaning relations within those categories. This organization enables us to instantly and automatically retrieve the words we need to carry on communication and to quickly understand words in a stream of speech as we hear it.

In *Word and Rules: The Ingredients of Language,* Steven Pinker discusses the speed with which each person can retrieve words from one's mental lexicon. He reports that when we listen and read, we search our mental lexicons and in less than one second recognize a real word or reject an unknown one. We can find the words that we need when speaking or writing with equally impressive speed.[19] Jean Aitchison has created a metaphor of words as two-sided coins—with the word's meaning and grammatical form on one side and sounds on the other—to represent word storage in the mental lexicon.[20] Words are organized in semantic categories for speaking and writing and by sound similarity for listening and for reading. Both sides of the coin have implications for classroom instruction, as described next.

Two instructional procedures for developing vocabulary based on semantic categories in the mental lexicon gained wide popularity among teachers in the 1980s, and that popularity has continued to this day. These procedures are *semantic mapping* or *webbing*[21] and *semantic feature analysis*.

Semantic Mapping

Semantic maps (also called *word webs, word maps,* and *concept maps*) are graphic organizers that present related words to show the nature of the meaning relationships between the words and a central concept. Semantic maps reflect the organization of words in the mental lexicon. Figure 4.1 is a partial semantic map related to the central concept *money*.

The semantic mapping procedure involves the following steps:

First, the teacher selects a central concept of pedagogical interest or importance, writes it where all can see it, and draws several lines outward, similar to the spokes of a wheel.

Second, the teacher writes category labels at the end of each line and lists some words in each category.

Third, the students are instructed to individually think about this concept, search their memories, and list as many additional related words as possible on their graphic of the semantic map.

Fourth, the teacher creates a class semantic map by adding words the students have suggested as well as others that the teacher feels are important to the central concept.

Finally, the teacher leads a class discussion about the word meanings that illustrates how the words are alike and different and indicates which words or meanings are new to some students.

The semantic map may be used as an outline or a guide for writing about the central topic of a lesson or activity. Some words on the map

What We Do with Money	Forms of Money
spend	coins
count	charge cards
squander	checks
purchase	money orders
save	bills
hoard	bonds
increase	coupons

MONEY

Ways to Get Money	Where We Keep Money
sell things	wallet
allowance	purse
loans	cash register
labor	safe
inherit	bank
find	pocket
gifts	money belt

FIGURE 4.1 **Partial Semantic Map for Money**

	motor	pedals	enclosed	driver's license	runners	2 wheel	4 wheel	passenger	driver stands	fare	horse drawn
automobile	+	-	+	+	-	-	+	+	-	-	-
skateboard	-	-	-	-	-	-	+	-	+	-	-
moped	+	+	-	+	-	+	-	-	-	-	-
sleigh	-	-	-	-	+	-	-	+	-	-	+
motorcycle	+	+	-	+	-	+	-	+	-	-	-
dogsled	-	-	-	-	+	-	-	+	+	-	-
bicycle	-	+	-	-	-	+	-	?	-	-	-
taxicab	+	-	+	+	-	-	+	+	-	+	-
unicycle	-	+	-	-	-	-	-	-	+	-	-
train	+	-	+	+	-	-	-	+	-	+	-

FIGURE 4.2 **Partial Semantic Grid for Conveyances**

will be relevant to the upcoming selection being read by the class. When engaged in semantic mapping, students not only learn new words and new meanings but also see the relationships among words tied to the semantic organization of their mental lexicons.

Semantic Feature Analysis

Semantic feature analysis is another practice that builds on and expands categories of words related to a central concept. Semantic feature grids are graphic organizers that have a list of words from the same semantic category on one side and a list of the semantic features of those words across the top. This format is illustrated in Figure 4.2, which features a partially complete semantic feature grid for the category *conveyances*.

Semantic feature analysis involves having the teacher and students list as many related words and descriptive features of the central concept as they can think of and for which there is space on a classroom board or a copy of a blank semantic grid. The class decides, through discussion, if a word on the left has one of the features across the top and, if so, they record a plus sign (+) in the box. If the feature is not characteristic of a word, a minus sign (-) is recorded. If there is uncertainty, a question mark (?) is recorded. By discussing the patterns of pluses and minuses, the students apprehend the uniqueness of each word in the category. Semantic feature grids are especially useful for teaching central concepts in the social studies and the sciences. The effectiveness of semantic mapping and semantic feature analysis is supported by several studies.[22]

Activities that focus on the similarities and differences in words within semantic categories are based on the meaning relations exemplified earlier. Such activities are based on word synonyms, antonyms, hyponyms (members or examples of a category), meronyms (parts), and attributes (descriptive features).

Synonyms are words that have similar meanings. The context of a sentence usually determines whether a synonym is appropriate. We might admire a person who is *witty* but not one who is *silly*. Which might we find more threatening, a *crowd* or a *mob*? When students understand that context influences which synonym is the best fit, they can better appreciate semantic nuances as they learn and use language.

Instructional Activity   4.1

This activity requires older students, alone or in groups, to create appropriate sentences for the two synonyms in a pair (e.g., "The (<u>mischievous</u>) child played an April Fool's Day prank" and "The (<u>vicious</u>) person hit the lizard with a stick"). The following synonymous pairs lend themselves to this sentence-construction activity. Students can be encouraged to use a dictionary or a thesaurus if required. The synonym must be appropriate to the situation in the sentence they create.

1. helpful
   overbearing
2. surprised
   flabbergasted
3. despondent
   unhappy
4. ask
   beg
5. tease
   torment
6. drink
   guzzle
7. suspend
   expel
8. spend
   squander
9. unfortunate
   tragic
10. irritated
    enraged
11. borrower
    leech
12. debate
    squabble
13. candid
    blunt
14. shy
    fearful
15. furious
    angry

Upon completion of this exercise, each group can try out its new sentences on the other students in the class by asking them which synonym best fits the sentence. For example: The synonyms are *debate* and *squabble*. Which word best fits this sentence? Why?

1. *The class continued to _____ about the new seating assignments.*
2. *Tomorrow we will continue the _____ about the presidential candidates.*

Next, have the students create sentences that show the difference between three synonymous words. As always, a discussion of responses can be instructive for all students.

1. appreciate
   value
   cherish
2. boast
   brag
   crow
3. risky
   dangerous
   hazardous
4. spoiled
   decayed
   rotten
5. wish
   desire
   crave
6. dirty
   filthy
   squalid
7. questionable
   doubtful
   dubious
8. humorous
   funny
   hilarious
9. flaw
   error
   blunder
10. strange
    bizarre
    grotesque
11. follow
    chase
    pursue
12. peer
    gaze
    stare

Exercises such as those above help learners appreciate the shades of differences among synonyms with nearly the same meaning.

─── **4.1**

Students of all ages have a tendency to overuse some words to the exclusion of synonyms that might better fit their context. Just as synonymous words are linked in our mental lexicons, a good thesaurus links synonymous and other related words. To the speaker or writer who wants to be more inventive, a thesaurus is an essential resource. To the language user who wants to venture beyond such words as *interesting, big,* and *nice,* a thesaurus offers *gripping, riveting, captivating, spellbinding; enormous, mammoth, gigantic, towering; pleasant, gracious,* and *congenial.*

There are other examples, too, of words used so often that they are tiresome to writer and reader alike. Using an elementary thesaurus, even younger students can compile lists of synonyms for the following words: *little, happy, sad, mad, walk, sit, good, look, eat, think, laugh, noise.* The students then can write and compare stories or poems using the various synonyms that they have compiled from their thesaurus.

Instructional Activity 4.2

Antonyms are words that have opposite meanings, and synonyms have meanings that may differ somewhat from one another based on sentence context. The following exercise requires older students to write sentences or create dialogues that indicate the difference between the synonym and antonym in a category. Students will find a dictionary helpful with this activity. As an example of a category target word, consider the adverb *loudly.* In the sentence *The band marched noisily down the street, but we could hear it only faintly from our twentieth-floor apartment,* the synonym of *loudly* is *noisily* and the antonym of *loudly* is *faintly.* Students can use either the synonym (S) or antonym (A) given to complete their sentences in the exercise.

Category	Adverbs	
1. crossly	(S) scornfully	irritably
	(A) cheerfully	buoyantly
2. carelessly	(S) thoughtlessly	mindlessly
	(A) cautiously	meticulously
3. slightly	(S) barely	weakly
	(A) robustly	fully
4. lovingly	(S) fondly	tenderly
	(A) grudgingly	hatefully
5. sternly	(S) severely	rigidly
	(A) gently	flexibly
6. gloomily	(S) moodily	sullenly
	(A) joyfully	lightly
7. anxiously	(S) fretfully	apprehensively
	(A) calmly	peacefully

A second antonym exercise requires that students have access to a thesaurus. Early in elementary school, students learn that antonyms are words with opposite meanings. In this chapter, we have shown that there are at least three categories of "oppositeness": gradable antonyms (e.g., *huge—minuscule*), complementary antonyms (e.g., *open—closed*), and converse antonyms (e.g., *parent—child*). Using their thesaurus, groups of students can compile a continuum of words from *most* to *least* for the following pairs of gradable antonyms:[23]

1. happy—sad
2. dark—light
3. heavy—light
4. exorbitant—cheap
5. cry—laugh
6. fast—slow
7. strong—weak
8. brave—fearful
9. hard—easy
10. loud—soft
11. good—bad
12. alert—tired

4.2

Analogies are comparisons of two things that are similar in some respects but different in others. In the analogy *swim* is to *pool* as *run* is to *track*, *swim* and *run* are similar in that they are athletic activities but they differ in the places where each is done (i.e., *pool* and *track*).

Instructional Activity 4.3

Here's an antonym analogy activity that is especially challenging. To complete the analogy, you must think of a word that is an antonym of the third italicized word and that rhymes with the second italicized word, as shown in this example: *Fierce* is to *gentle* as *physical* is to *mental*.[24] With this activity, a thesaurus and a rhyming dictionary can be helpful resources. The correct answers for the following items are at the end of the chapter.

1. *Support* is to *balk* as *peek* is to _____.
2. *Capture* is to *release* as *decline* is to _____.
3. *Interesting* is to *boring* as *ceiling* is to _____.
4. *Start* is to *complete* as *advance* is to _____.
5. *Heavy* is to *light* as *weakness* is to _____.
6. *Spicier* is to *blander* as *praise* is to _____.
7. *Smooth* is to *creaky* as *straightforward* is to _____.
8. *Lesser* is to *greater* as *hill* is to _____.
9. *Warmth* is to *chilliness* as *wisdom* is to _____.
10. *Good* is to *naughty* as *modest* is to _____.

In a small group, create additional rhyming antonym analogies. You might want to use a thesaurus and a rhyming dictionary as resources.

4.3

Instructional Activity 4.4

In this activity, you will work with a partner to examine pairs of words (e.g., *estate, ranch*) and discuss how the words are alike and how they are different. *Estate* and *ranch* are alike, for example, because they both are residences with large acreage, but they are different in that *ranches* are used for raising animals and *estates* usually are not used for this purpose. A dictionary will be helpful with some words in this activity.

1. *hangar—boathouse*
2. *gazebo—cabana*
3. *closet—armoire*
4. *gable—eave*
5. *doorway—hatch*
6. *arboretum—conservatory*
7. *dean—provost*
8. *bayou—swamp*
9. *cafeteria—delicatessen (deli)*
10. *moth—butterfly*
11. *counter—table*
12. *tulip—tuberose*
13. *flower pot—planter*
14. *hurricane—tornado*
15. *glass—beaker*
16. *clarinet—oboe*

4·4

Instructional Activity 4.5

In this related activity, students are asked to identify the one word that does not belong with the other words in the set. That word is not a member (i.e., hyponym) of the category or a part (i.e., meronym) of the category label.

For example, in the set *peach, potato, pineapple,* and *pear, potato* does not fit because it is a vegetable and the others are fruits. In the set *wrapper, seeds, skin,* and *pulp, wrapper* does not belong because, unlike the others, *wrapper* is not a part of a fruit. Find the word that does not belong with the others and explain why it does not fit. Answers are at the end of the chapter.

1. *skiff, scow, scooter, pontoon*
2. *cumin, rutabaga, paprika, nutmeg*
3. *bovine, carp, gar, sardine*
4. *glossary, dictionary, lexicon, entry*
5. *chef, patron, sommelier, maitre d'*
6. *freesia, liatris, dispenser, anemone*
7. *czar, king, president, queen*
8. *bumper, dashboard, hubcap, fender*
9. *sound, word, phrase, sentence*
10. *flannel, denim, chiffon, carafe*

This activity can be undertaken even with very young children if you use pictures of the objects (e.g., *eagle, jet, elephant, kite*). And for older students, you can use a Venn diagram—consisting of two intersecting circles—with more sophisticated words (e.g., *recession, depression*). Here, you might list characteristics of *recession* in the left third of the diagram, those of *depression* in the right third, and shared characteristics in the overlapping center.

4.5

Word Categories

Instructional activities that help students acquire new words and new meanings for known words through classification tasks are well supported in the research literature. Classification is a basic mental process that undergirds all learning: People learn to the degree that they can relate new knowledge to prior knowledge. The effectiveness of classification on vocabulary learning and recall has been demonstrated in numerous studies.[25] Classification activities involve the systematic arrangement of words and ideas into categories formed by predetermined criteria. School-aged children have had years of experience in the semantic classification of concepts and words. The three main tasks in word learning are naming, classifying, and relating to the world around us. This chapter has focused on the semantic categories and networks within our language and their reality in each individual's mental lexicon.

Answers to Instructional Activity 4.3

1. gawk	2. increase
3. flooring	4. retreat
5. might	6. slander
7. sneaky	8. crater
9. silliness	10. haughty

Answers to Instructional Activity 4.5

1. A *scooter* is not a type of boat.
2. A *rutabaga* is not a spice.
3. *Bovine* is not a fish.
4. An *entry* is not a list.
5. A *patron* usually is not a restaurant employee.
6. A *dispenser* is not a flower.
7. A *president* is elected, the others are not.
8. A *dashboard* is inside a car.
9. *Sound* is not a unit of meaning.
10. A *carafe* is not a type of cloth.

Notes

1. Susan Kelz Sperling, *Poplollies & Bellibones: A Celebration of Lost Words* (Old Saybrook, CT: Konecky & Konecky, 1977), p. 101.

2. Barbara Ann Kipfer, ed., *Roget's International Thesaurus: Revised and Updated*, 6th ed. (New York: HarperCollins, 2001).

3. Anne H. Soukanov and Kathy Rooney, eds., *Encarta World English Dictionary* (New York: St. Martin's Press, 1999).

4. Dale D. Johnson, *Vocabulary in the Elementary and Middle School* (Needham Heights, MA: Allyn & Bacon, 2001).

5. Eve V. Clark, *The Lexicon in Acquisition*, Cambridge Studies in Linguistics (Cambridge, UK: Cambridge University Press, 1993).

6. William E. Nagy and Richard C. Anderson, "How Many Words Are There in Printed School English?" *Reading Research Quarterly* 19 (1984): 304–330.

7. Michael F. Graves, "Vocabulary Learning and Instruction," in *Review of Research in Education*, ed. Edward Rothkopf, 49–89 (Washington, DC: American Educational Research Association, 1986).

8. Ibid.; Jean Aitchison, *Words in the Mind: An Introduction to the Mental Lexicon*, 2nd ed. (Oxford, UK: Blackwell, 1994).

9. David Crystal, *The Cambridge Encyclopedia of the English Language* (Cambridge, UK: Cambridge University Press, 1995).

10. Kipfer, *Roget's International Thesaurus*.

11. Stephen Glazier, *Random House Word Menu* (New York: Random House, 1992).

12. Kay Christian, and others, eds., *Historical Thesaurus of the Oxford English Dictionary* (Oxford, UK: Oxford University Press, 2009).

13. Crystal, *The Cambridge Encyclopedia of the English Language*.

14. Clark, *The Lexicon in Acquisition*.

15. Ibid., p. 9.

16. George A. Miller, *The Science of Words* (New York: Scientific American Library, 1996).

17. G. H. Kent and A. J. Rosanoff, "A Study of Association," *American Journal of Insanity* 6 (1910): 156.

18. Miller, *The Science of Words*, pp. 156–157.

19. Steven Pinker, *Word and Rules: The Ingredients of Language* (New York: Perennial, 1999), p. 3.

20. Aitchison, *Words in the Mind*, p. 222.

21. Ibid.; Dale D. Johnson and P. David Pearson, *Teaching Reading Vocabulary* (Fort Worth, TX: Holt, Rinehart and Winston, 1978 [reprinted in 1984]).

22. See, among others, Johnson and Pearson, *Teaching Reading Vocabulary*; Anne-Marie Cornu, "The First Step in Vocabulary Teaching," *Modern Language Journal* 63 (1979): 262–272; and Ronald Carter, *Vocabulary: Applied Linguistic Perspectives* (New York: Routledge, 1987).

23. For example, a continuum for the antonym pair *wail—howl* could be *wail, cry, weep, whimper, frown, smile, chuckle, laugh, howl.*

24. Bonnie Johnson, *Wordworks: Exploring Language Play* (Golden, CO: Fulcrum Publishing, 1999), p. 135.

25. See, for example, Walter Kintsch and T. A. van Dijk, "Toward a Model of Text Comprehension and Production," *Psychological Review* 85 (1978): 363–394; Aitchison, *Words in the Mind*;, Miller, *The Science of Words*; and Steven A. Stahl and Katherine A. Stahl, "Word Wizards All!" in *Vocabulary Instruction: Research to Practice*, ed. James F. Baumann and Edward J. Kame´enui, 59–78 (New York: Guilford Press, 2004).

Ambiguity in Language

5

The ambiguous headlines below are examples of how words that have more than one definition, such as *suit* and *dense*, can cause confusion in written or spoken messages.

> *Lawyer Presents Argument in Peanut Suit*
> *Mayor Blames Dense Population for Traffic Woes*

Our language is loaded with multiple-meaning words. A classic study published in 1983 found that 72 percent of common words used in children's trade books and schoolbooks have multiple meanings.[1] That percentage has increased since then because additional meanings for existing words are added to American English each year (e.g., *window* now can refer to *caller ID*).

Even seemingly straightforward, user-friendly words such as *dog* and *up* have many meanings. *Dog* means *an animal that barks, a fortunate human* (You lucky dog), *not good* (That movie is a dog), *to follow or pester someone* (Bad luck seems to dog the team), and *a Greyhound bus.* The word *dog* also is a part of:

> *dog-eat-dog* (highly competitive) [*It's a dog-eat-dog business.*]
>
> *dog-eared* (creased, worn out) [*The pages of the book are dog-eared.*]
>
> *dog-gone* (irritating, annoying) [*That dog-gone alarm clock rings too early.*]
>
> *doggy bag* (customer bag for leftovers) [*Martha asked the server for a doggy bag.*]
>
> *dog paddle* (a swimming stroke) [*The dog paddle is not used in competitive swimming.*]
>
> *dog tag* (military tag on a neck chain worn for identification) [*My mother kept her old dog tags in her dresser.*]
>
> *dog-and-pony show* (a grand production that is meant to impress) [*When the inspectors came around, we had to put on a dog-and-pony show.*]
>
> *go to the dogs* (to decline in quality) [*If our budget gets cut any further, our department will go to the dogs.*]
>
> *put on the dog* (to show off with expensive things) [*The Smiths always put on the dog at country club parties.*]
>
> *dog tired* (exhausted) [*At the end of the school year, I was dog tired.*]
>
> *watchdog* (a guard dog or a person who monitors a group and looks for questionable activities) [*Jack is the watchdog of the association.*]
>
> *underdog* (someone not expected to succeed) [*She likes to support the underdog.*]
>
> *top dog* (the person with the most influence or power) [*The top dog usually gets the most pay.*]
>
> *sick as a dog* (ill but usually not with a terminal disease) [*When I had the flu bug, I was sick as a dog.*]
>
> *hot dog* (a frankfurter or one who performs daring athletic stunts or an expression of enthusiasm) [*"Hot dog!" said the hot dog as he jumped from the plane.*]
>
> *hangdog* (sad or guilty looking) [*Willie had a hangdog expression when he lost the account.*]

dog days of summer (hot, humid days of summer) [*It's mid-August, and the dog days of summer are here.*]

call off the dogs (to stop criticizing someone) [*She's innocent, so it's time to call off the dogs.*]

Many more examples could be added to the preceding list. *Up* can mean:

at a higher level (We climbed *up* the mountain.)

out (They pulled *up* the tomatoes when they froze.)

winning by (The Packers are *up* by fourteen points.)

happening, going on (What's *up* with Maria?)

move closer (Move *up* so you can see the screen.)

was mentioned (The subject came *up* near the end of the meeting.)

to make louder (She turns the sound *up* when the commercials are over.)

to rise (The sun is *up*.)

to move along (Go *up* the path until you come to the waterfall.)

expiring (Our lease is *up* in October.)

thoroughly completed (The agent tore the contract *up*.)

running for something (He is *up* for a Grammy award.)

operating correctly (Is the computer *up* and running?)

turn (Who's *up* next?)

honest (That realtor is on the *up* and *up*.)

facing (Claire is *up* against a challenge.)

move suddenly (Please don't *up* and leave.)

capable of doing (Mr. Santez is *up* to the job.)

causing suspicion (What's he *up* to?)

ready for (I'm *up* for some pizza.)

Up has other meanings as well: *up for grabs* (available to anyone), *up front* (in advance or honest), *up the creek* (in trouble), *sent up the river* (sent to jail), *up one's alley* (appealing to that person), *up in arms* (angry), *up in the air* (not certain), *up one's sleeve* (something held in reserve), *up and at 'em* (get out of bed), *up to here with* (tired of something or someone), and *up-to-the-minute* (very recent).

The linguistic term for multiple meanings is *polysemy* (pah-LISS-uh-mee). Some polysemous words such as *run, take, set,* and *stand* have hundreds of meanings.[2] Some polysemous words have meanings that are "close." Tom McArthur points out that "*walk* (action), *walk* (street [as in 75 Maple Walk]) are relatively close, but *crane* (bird), *crane* (machine) are much farther apart."[3] And as Jean Aitchison notes:

> The word *old* is an old problem. Consider: Pauline was astonished to see—
> —an old woman (an aged woman)
> —an old friend (a long-standing friend)
> —her old boyfriend (former boyfriend)
> —old Fred (Fred whom she knew well)

The old woman is aged, but the others may be young. The old friend is still a friend, but the old boyfriend might now be an enemy. . . . In the case of *old Fred*, English speakers have to know that *old* attached to proper names is a mark of friendly affection.[4]

Perhaps the most reasonable way for a teacher to address multiple-meaning words is to remind students, as they learn words, that most words in our language have more than one meaning. If, for example, the word *scallops* is part of a social studies lesson on marine life, a teacher might point out that *to scallop* means *to make a wavy edge with a scissors or other implement* and that *scalloped* potatoes are made with milk and flour. The various meanings might not stick with the students the first time around, but through this type of vocabulary instruction they will develop a mindset for multiple meanings.

There are two principal types of ambiguity—lexical and grammatical. Lexical ambiguity refers to the multiple meanings of words. In the sentence *Wally is good at making chips*, the possible meanings are that Wally is skilled at making chip shots in golf, Wally knows how to turn out tasty potato chips, or Wally is adept at making computer components.

Grammatical ambiguity can be seen in a sentence such as *Visiting relatives can be fun*, which can mean either that it is enjoyable when relatives come to visit or that it is fun to visit relatives. The same sort of ambiguity can be found in *Jenny likes fine automobiles and motorcycles*. This sentence could mean that Jenny likes only superb automobiles and superb motorcycles or that Jenny likes fine automobiles and any kind of motorcycle. *They can fish* could mean that they know how to fish, have permission to fish, or know how to preserve fish in cans.

Can you spot the ambiguities in the sentences below?

Biting dogs can be dangerous.
Ms. Knutson likes to have discussions with intelligent students and
    colleagues.
They are cooking apples.
Flying planes can cause nervousness.

Instructional Activity 5.1

This activity is designed for use in the elementary grades. Teachers begin discussions of multiple-meaning words early in these grades. They tell pupils that some words can mean more than one thing. They find pictures (or draw pictures if they can) that illustrate two different meanings for simple, easy-to-decode words. The target words are used in sentences to provide context for the pupils. If students are unable to read the sentences independently, the sentences are read orally by the teacher and then repeated by the pupils and teacher as the teacher points to each word. A discussion of each sentence and its plausibility follows each pair. Several examples are given in Figures 5.1 through 5.4.

Some elementary pupils, with assistance, will be able to write and illustrate their own examples of multiple-meaning words in sentences. Simple sentences such as *A dog is running into a pen* and *We saw a school of fish* should be used. Other suitable words for this activity include *band, bark, block, glasses, hand, horns, scale, snap, tag,* and *wave*.

1. The <u>bat</u> flew into the cave.

2. We measured the box with a <u>ruler</u>.

3. That student is <u>bright</u>.

4. Carl took a <u>step</u> toward the door.

5. Our <u>coach</u> said that we played a good game.

FIGURE 5.1

1. Mr. Holis likes <u>wild</u> strawberries.

2. Ruby walked a <u>block</u> to the store.

3. That clock's <u>ring</u> is loud.

4. We took the car back to the dealer because it was a <u>lemon</u>.

5. The bull will <u>charge</u> the scarecrow.

FIGURE 5.2

1. Monica is <u>testing</u> the soup.

2. That elephant's <u>trunk</u> can reach high places.

3. Tim put <u>letters</u> into the mailbox.

4. Mr. Harris lives on the second <u>story</u>.

5. The tiny bird slept on the <u>perch</u>.

FIGURE 5.3

1. The painter put another <u>coat</u> on the wall.

2. Jan's goat has two <u>horns</u>.

3. That <u>star</u> won many awards.

4. Peter will <u>serve</u> the ball.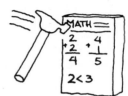

5. The math worksheet is <u>hard</u>.

FIGURE 5.4

Instructional Activity 5.2

It is not difficult to locate ambiguous headlines in print media. *Doing Business on the Green* was a recent headline in *USA Today*. The article described resort hotels where business is conducted on golf courses. *Using Their Noodles* was a headline in an Elkhart, Indiana, newspaper. The article introduced a new noodle-making factory in that state.

Intermediate students can create their own ambiguous headlines from a list of multiple-meaning words provided by the teacher. Following are several examples of ambiguous headlines. Some intermediate students will enjoy illustrating and explaining both the intended and unintended meanings of each headline.

Board Approves Raises
Airport to Be Built on South Bank
New Bill Introduced in Congress
Jewels Found by Picnic Table
Chicago Plant on Strike
Leader Sticks to Plan
Cattle Moved from Range
Band Chooses Olive Uniforms
Jam Delays Parade
Mints on Pillows a Favorite Hotel Treat
Chair Resigns at Meeting
Racket Upsets Neighbors
Governor Throws Party
Pollution Stunts Cones
Bumper Crop Is Harvested
Blizzard Sweeps Midwest
Garcia Joins Cast on Stage
International Visitor Orders Pizza to Go
Team Catches Bus
Evening News to Get New Anchor

Boat Drawing Today
Fans Gather at Stage Door
Robber's Short Sentence Angers Community
Jury Hears Testimony in Tuba Case
Local Man Mentioned in Author's Appendix
Wise Eaters Turn to Fruit

5.2

Instructional Activity 5.3

Older students can participate in a nonsense substitution activity. For this exercise, the teacher divides the class into groups of three. Students are given a list of multiple-meaning words such as *base, bit, bluff, dash, dull, general, match, rare,* and *stock*. They then write groups of sentences using the same multiple-meaning word in each group. Next, the students create several nonsense words (e.g., *blifs, flun, nif, plarn*) and replace the multiple-meaning word in the group of sentences with a particular nonsense word, as exemplified in the sample sentences below. Groups guess each other's target multiple-meaning words.

1. She dug a *flun* in the field for the excess water.
2. A *flun* is a type of waterway.
3. He needs to *flun* his energy into something worthwhile.
4. That television *flun* has too many commercials.
(*Flun* is *channel.*)
1. The *nif* of that book is clever.
2. *Nif* the plants tonight.
3. Put a plastic *nif* on that.
4. Take *nif* or you will get wet.
(*Nif* is *cover.*)
1. She bought a jewelry *plarn* for her mother.
2. It was a *plarn* of poison ivy.
3. The *plarn* was argued by a new attorney.

4. In *plarn* it is cold, take your gloves.
(*Plarn* is *case.*)
1. That machine can *mip* olives.
2. You do not have to *mip* that scarf.
3. The *mip* gave the incident a lot of attention.
4. That *mip* sells only history books.
(*Mip* is *press.*)
1. There is a *slun* of fog over the valley.
2. He has a *slun* on his sleeve.
3. The spinach *slun* is dry.
4. Did you *slun* it up with your friend?
(*Slun* is *patch.*)
1. The *blifs* were stale.
2. That vase has little *blifs* in it.
3. When the *blifs* are down, we try even harder.
4. Those kids are *blifs* off the old block.
(*Blifs* is *chips.*)

5.3

In the preceding twenty-four sentences, the context often points the way to the intended meanings.

Every school subject and every occupation has multiple-meaning words in its vocabularies. Here are some examples:

School Subjects
English: *appendix, article, colon, construction, objective, particle, possessive, root, sentence, stem, subject, tense*
History: *bill, cabinet, colony, court, crown, draft, frame, general, league, party, register, sail, space, stamp, train*

Occupations
Chef: *batter, cake, dash, date, dress, grill, ground, measure, mold, pan, range, season, sheet, stew, stock, wrap*

Realtor: *code, cooperative, deed, interest, listing, lot, parcel, points, principal, superintendent, survey, title*

Have small groups of older students select a school subject or an occupation and tell them to list as many multiple-meaning words as they can within a reasonable amount of time. Groups can present their lists to the class. As they do so, they can ask volunteers to give two or more meanings for each word on their lists, or the groups can ask students to write sentences in which the context suggests the meanings of the multiple-meaning words.

Instructional Activity   5.4

Older students also enjoy "A Second Meaning." In this activity, small groups are given a multiple-meaning word and one of the definitions or a clue to the meaning. Their task, through discussion, is to come up with a second definition or a clue to a second definition for the word. The groups may use a dictionary. The first five items in the list below are examples. Possible answers for the remaining items are at the end of the chapter.

Meaning	Multiple-Meaning Word	Meaning
1. actors	cast	*broken bone support*
2. to fool	bluff	*a cliff*
3. to swim	dip	*sauce for potato chips*
4. to run quickly	dash	*a punctuation mark*
5. use hammer	pound	*sixteen ounces*
6. shrub or tree	plant	
7. corn	crop	
8. crushing sound	crunch	
9. hot dog	frank	
10. piece of cookware	pan	
11. ship	vessel	
12. tired	sleeper	

13. lather	soap
14. thermometer	degrees
15. thread	needle
16. candidates	ticket
17. to not sink	float
18. furniture	table
19. a feeling	hunch
20. trees used for wood	lumber
21. empty	hollow
22. art, music, theater	culture
23. fence	picket
24. plug	outlet
25. suitcase	pack
26. leaf	stem
27. not a success	flop
28. red dots	rash
29. wet land	swamp
30. clock	alarm

5.4

Instructional Activity 5.5

A variation of the prior activity is "Two Meanings," in which the students, working in groups, must supply two meanings—or clues to two meanings—for the multiple-meaning word. The students may use a dictionary. As before, the first five list items are examples. Possible answers for the remaining items are at the end of the chapter.

Meaning	Multiple-Meaning Word	Meaning
31. *medical care*	patient	*to wait calmly*
32. *farm land*	field	*occupation*

33. *bird*	duck	*to bend down quickly*
34. *official clothing*	uniform	*same weight and size*
35. *lightning*	bolt	*to run fast*
36.	company	
37.	customs	
38.	curb	
39.	tie	
40.	sink	
41.	spine	
42.	lemon	
43.	rich	
44.	rung	
45.	fine	
46.	lace	
47.	carp	
48.	bit	
49.	draw	
50.	panel	
51.	draft	
52.	gouge	
53.	loaf	
54.	dart	
55.	match	
56.	wrench	
57.	key	
58.	joint	
59.	stern	
60.	screen	

5.5

Instructional Activity 5.6

"Name the Multiple-Meaning Word" is a challenging activity that requires students to read or listen to clue words and phrases and then name the multiple-meaning word that fits those clue words or phrases. For example, if the clue word and phrase are *strange* and *one and three*, the multiple-meaning word is *odd*. If the clue words are *door* and *map*, the multiple-meaning word is *key*. Below are forty pairs of clue words and phrases. Once again, the first five are examples. Possible answers to the remaining items are at the end of the chapter.

Meaning	Multiple-Meaning Word	Meaning
61. small piece	*scrap*	to give up on something
62. to rush	*scramble*	to mix something up
63. horns	*brass*	copper and zinc
64. glue	*cement*	to make stronger
65. quickly	*fast*	held tightly
66. thin thread		vegetables, fruit, grains
67. not straight		thin
68. a table		tree part
69. a type of wrapping		to stop
70. to preserve		to make better
71. to crush		acorn and zucchini
72. average		nasty
73. code		none
74. list of names		small loaf
75. long tale		sweater
76. big truck		oil
77. tiny amount		to squeeze
78. piece of land		main theme

79. not often

red or pink

80. to make jittery

baby's toy

81. secret listening

germ

82. less expensive seat

trainer

83. to smile

big piece of wood

84. special equipment

landing

85. fruit juice

tool for making
small holes

86. disease

to cause trouble
repeatedly

87. to become stuck

gathering place

88. price increase

a long walk

89. decoration

given in addition to
pay

90. chair and table

part of a trip

91. goat and rhino

car and truck

92. dry throat

amphibian

93. used on stage

to support

94. sea animal

get something
without work

95. to waste money
or time

covered with flour
and eggs

96. butter and cream
cheese

big farm or ranch

97. a supply

liquid for soups

98. big basket

to make more
difficult to do

99. wheat and corn

a small piece

100. to weaken

maple syrup

5.6

American English is replete with multiple-meaning words and syntactic ambiguity. If students are not alert to the probability of encountering

such ambiguities, their listening and reading comprehension can be affected. Learning to anticipate that most words have more than one meaning, and then determining the author's or speaker's intended meaning, can be a challenge to all readers—but especially to English-language learners (ELLs). There is a great diversity among ELLs with respect to their primary language, country of origin, cultural heritage, prior knowledge, educational experiences, and English-language proficiencies. All of these differing cognitive-linguistic and experiential factors are brought to the reading task by English-language learners. Solving language ambiguity problems, however, need not be drudgery as we have attempted to illustrate in this chapter.

Possible Answers to Instructional Activity 5.4

6. factory
7. to cut short
8. tight bind
9. honest
10. criticize severely
11. container
12. unexpectedly good
13. TV serial
14. academic
15. tease
16. entrance pass
17. parade exhibit
18. postpone
19. bent over
20. move sluggishly
21. valley
22. biological specimen
23. demonstration
24. discount store
25. group of dogs
26. stop
27. lie down heavily
28. reckless
29. inundate
30. frighten

Possible Answers to Instructional Activity 5.5

36. a firm, guests
37. traditions, duty
38. pavement edge, stop
39. a draw, tighten laces
40. basin, submerge
41. backbone, courage
42. citrus fruit, bad product
43. wealthy, highly caloric
44. ladder step, did ring
45. very thin, a fee
46. delicate fabric, thread through holes
47. fish, complain
48. small amount, binary digit
49. illustrate, unholster

50. deliberative group, rectangular board

51. rough copy, air current

52. overcharge, dig hole

53. baked bread, do nothing

54. move quickly, pointed missile

55. good pair, ignitor

56. yank, tool

57. main point, locking device

58. jail, connection

59. strict, back of ship

60. mesh protector, select

Possible Answers to Instructional Activity 5.6

66. fiber	67. lean	68. leaf
69. foil	70. cure	71. squash
72. mean	73. zip	74. roll
75. yarn	76. rig	77. pinch
78. plot	79. rare	80. rattle
81. bug	82. coach	83. beam
84. gear	85. punch	86. plague
87. lodge	88. hike	89. fringe
90. leg	91. horn	92. frog
93. prop	94. sponge	95. fritter
96. spread	97. stock	98. hamper
99. grain	100. sap	

Notes

1. Dale D. Johnson and Alden J. Moe, *The Ginn Word Book for Teachers* (Lexington, MA: Ginn and Company, 1983).

2. Bonnie Johnson, *Wordworks: Exploring Language Play* (Golden, CO: Fulcrum Publishing, 1999).

3. Tom McArthur, *The Concise Oxford Companion to the English Language* (Oxford, UK: Oxford University Press, 1996), p. 715.

4. Jean Aitchison, *Words in the Mind: An Introduction to the Mental Lexicon*, 2nd ed. (Oxford, UK: Blackwell, 1994), p. 62.

Figurative Language

6

"You're a Sage, Rosemary"

Speakers and readers of American English would have no difficulties comprehending this tale as told by the indomitable Rosemary—even though it is peppered with figurative language:

I was born in the Big Apple and raised in Bean Town. I met Frank at a rubber chicken affair where we were packed in like sardines. We started to chew the fat, and I learned that he was a bean counter. I had a plum job working for a big cheese in the government. I helped her add pork to bills.

Frank seemed like a good egg—a smart cookie who could cut the mustard in a pressure cooker environment. After several months of dating, we decided to marry. The night we wed must have been an omen. The fog was as thick as pea soup and even though the terrain was as flat as a pancake, it took over an hour to get to the J.P.'s office.

Our first year together was just peachy. "Honey?" Frank would coo. "Yes, Dumpling," I'd respond. "Lamb Chop?" Frank would whisper. "Right here, Pumpkin," I'd murmur. We both were breadwinners so we were riding the gravy train, piling up the dough. "Life is a bowl of cherries," said clever Frank. Some weekends we'd fritter away our free time just vegging out. Other times we'd use the old beans to create detective stories. Our latest was about a chicken-livered protagonist who ran into a hard-boiled bad egg.

After five years of marriage, something was fishy. Frank started to act like a fruitcake. When he was home, he was a couch potato who would do nothing but beef about the eggheads he worked with. I thought he really was going bananas when he started reciting proverbs to me: "Man does not live by bread alone; fine words butter no parsnips." What a nut! I thought Frank was working too hard and tried to dangle a carrot in front of him—a week's vacation in Tahiti, but he responded like a wet noodle.

Eventually I heard through the grapevine that I was playing second banana. I decided to stalk Frank on his next outing to see for myself. This isn't sour grapes talking, but when I saw them together, they looked crummy. A string bean and a carrot-top shrimp. Comparing Frank's new sweetie pie and me was like comparing apples and oranges. I swallowed hard and drove home.

When Frank arrived, I didn't mince words. I told him to spill the beans about his little cupcake. "Don't try to sugar-coat the facts, Frank," I warned. "You were caught with your hand in the cookie jar." Frank turned beet red but remained as cool as a cucumber. "Don't clam up now," I yelled, "and don't fudge. The truth, Frank." He suggested that I simmer down, and then Frank told me the whole enchilada. He said he had wanted to sow some wild oats for the past year and he did. First there was Olive. Then came Ginger. After egging him on, Frank finally told me about "saucy little Pickles."

Frank tried to eat humble pie. He whimpered that he still loved me and would like to stay married, but I raged, "You're full of baloney, Frank. You're not worth a fig. You can't have your cake and eat it, too. I'm dropping you like a hot potato. I have bigger fish to fry. How do you like *them* apples?" Frank told me to simmer down, but I was boiling. "Now you're in a pickle, Frank!" I fumed. "Your goose is cooked." I gave him the raspberries and stormed out.

I had to take stock. You can't unscramble eggs. No sense loafing around, carping about Frank, and stewing over things I couldn't change. Now I'd be the only one bringing home the bacon so I decided to start a new career. On the first interview, I was grilled for an hour, and they wanted me to work for peanuts. The second interview was with some turkey who was as slow as molasses in January—an hour late for our meeting! All we talked about were trifles. I was steaming. The third try was a piece of cake. This was a new business with opportunities sprouting up every day and perks that could mushroom quickly. I would be in charge of selling used cars. It seemed like small potatoes for earning my bread and butter, but these cars were not lemons—just cream puffs. The icing on the cake was that I didn't have to butter up the customers because the cars were top shelf. They sold like hotcakes.

Oh, and my social life? Well, after Frank, I met Angus. He was too crusty—a crab. Butter wouldn't melt in his mouth. Then came Basil—too syrupy, a cornball, a ham. Sandwiched in between was sloppy Joe—worth a mint but masquerading as a po'boy. Finally, my Reuben appeared. He's the best thing since sliced bread. A real meat and potatoes kind of guy. We're two peas in a pod. Sometimes I rib Reuben, but he just smiles sweetly and says, "My little Honey Bun." I always have been a sucker for mush. "Here's a toast to you, Reuben, the world is our oyster," I say. "You're a sage, Rosemary," Reuben replies.[1]

It is not only narratives that use colorful words and phrases. Regardless of the topic being addressed, figurative language often will make an appearance. National and local print media, in paper and electronic form, are filled with figurative expressions:

"Jump on It Before You Kick"
  —*USA Today*
"For Some Foes the Chat, Some the Cold Shoulder"
  —*New York Times*
"Survey Pins Down Views on Patriotism"
  —*Green Bay Press Gazette*
"Ford Counts on Spruced Up F-150"
  —*USA Today*
"Investigators Put the Brakes on a Dimwitted Pair of Thieves . . ."
  —*New York Post*
"That Prospectus May Need a Fine Tooth Comb"
  —*New York Times*
"Too Often, Chief Executives Sugarcoat the Truth"
  —*Wall Street Journal*

We cannot be considered literate citizens unless we can understand figurative language.

David Crystal offers this definition of figurative language: "An expressive use of language where words are used in a nonliteral way to suggest illuminating comparisons and resemblances. . . . Literal language, by contrast, refers to the usual meanings of a word or phrase."[2] Theodore Harris and Richard Hodges provide a similar definition of figures of speech: "the expressive, nonliteral use of language for special effects, usually through images, as in metaphor and personification."[3] Determining precisely where literal ends and figurative begins is not always simple. In the simile *Karen was happy as a lark*, the comparison is clearly figurative. We have no idea how happy larks are. But in the simile *John's face was red as a beet*, the comparison could be literal or figurative. Tom McArthur has presented a summation of figurative language, and it will serve as a guide in this chapter:

> Classical rhetoric has tended to present figurative language as the concern primarily of poets, orators, critics, and language teachers, while conceding (usually in a brief aside) that everybody else uses it too and that the term therefore covers a universal practice in which sound, spelling, grammar, vocabulary, usage, and meaning are adapted to achieve special stylistic effects.[4]

Anthony Ortony argues for teaching figurative language to young children:

> It would not be unreasonable at this juncture to wonder why one should bother to introduce figurative uses of language to young children. . . . First, figurative language is a powerful way of relating old knowledge to new. Second, figurative language increases the expressive power of the available linguistic resources by permitting the expression of what might otherwise be difficult or impossible to express. How else can the opera singer's voice be described, if not by the metaphorical use of some word like *thin*? And if ships don't plow the seas, what do they do literally?[5]

In fact, Ortony urges teaching figurative language beginning in the early school grades rather than waiting until the middle grades as is typically done.

Figurative language has not always found its way into classroom instruction, but its importance has been recognized by some state departments of education. State standards in English and literacy call for:

" . . . the use of language subtleties in figurative language and idioms" (Colorado).

" . . . different elements of figurative language" (Florida).

the ability to "identify mood, tone, style and figurative language" (Idaho).

the ability to "write a story using some figurative language" (New York).

" . . . identifying and correctly using idioms and words with literal and figurative meanings" (Pennsylvania).

the ability to "consider the effects authors achieve through imagery and figurative language" (South Dakota).

In this chapter we describe, define, and exemplify seven figures of speech: *idioms, similes, metaphors, personification, euphemisms, hyperbole,* and *chiasmus.*

Idioms

Idioms are combinations of words that represent a unique meaning that cannot be inferred from the meanings of the individual words. For this reason, idioms are best learned in the same ways as individual words. *The red carpet treatment,* for example, means to treat a person in a way usually reserved for royalty or celebrities. Synonyms cannot be used in idiomatic expressions. *The red rug treatment* or *the maroon carpet treatment* are not considered to be idiomatic expressions.

Some idioms, as shown below, have been in use for centuries:[6]

Idiom	Meaning	Date of Origin
out of the woods	to have trouble behind us	200 B.C.
dirt cheap	not very expensive	60 A.D.
in one ear and out the other	to ignore what one hears	80 A.D.
at a snail's pace	to move slowly	1400
to be skin and bones	too thin	1430
too many irons in the fire	too many projects at once	1549
to smell a rat	to be highly suspicious	1550
to be in a pickle	to be in trouble	1585
to change one's tune	to change one's mind	1600
right under one's nose	clearly visible	1607
to have bigger fish to fry	to have more important things to do	1630
with flying colors	with great success	1692

Many familiar idioms originally had literal meanings. For example, *to know the ropes* meant to understand and master the complex system of ropes and cords used on ships centuries ago. As Olivia Isil notes, knowing the ropes was so indispensable that "discharge papers were once marked, 'knows the ropes,' thus constituting an honorable discharge."[7]

To give someone the cold shoulder also originally had a literal meaning. It was customary in the 1800s to serve an unwanted guest a less-than-choice shoulder piece of cold meat. The guest would realize that a warm meal was not forthcoming and there was no reason to dally. *To start from scratch*, or to start from the beginning, traces back to animal or human races in which the starting line was scratched into the ground. *To strike while the iron is hot* can be traced to the Middle Ages, when blacksmiths had to form the iron they were working with before it cooled and hardened. *Baker's dozen*, or thirteen of something, also was used in the Middle Ages. Scales were not accurate during that time, so to avoid punishment for selling baked goods that were underweight, bakers tossed in an extra item for every dozen sold.

Acclaimed writers throughout history have coined or used idioms in their works. Here are just a few examples: William Shakespeare (*green-eyed monster*), John Milton (*add fuel to the fire*), Jonathan Swift (*do not darken my door*), Sir Walter Scott (*to catch someone red-handed*), Edgar Allan Poe (*to go by the book*), Charles Dickens (*behind the times*), Mark Twain (*food for thought*), and Winston Churchill (*business as usual*).

American English contains a plentiful supply of synonymous idioms.[8] For example:

> Idioms for *in trouble*: *in a jam, in a pickle, in hot water, in a tight spot, in the doghouse.*
>
> Idioms for *similarity*: *in the same boat, speak the same language, two peas in a pod.*
>
> Idioms for *angry*: *burned up, fit to be tied, hot under the collar, to see red.*
>
> Idioms for *escape*: *break loose, cut and run, fly the coop, give someone the slip, make a run for it.*
>
> Idioms for *searching*: *dig something up, go on a fishing expedition, go over something with a fine-toothed comb, hunt high and low, leave no stone unturned, poke around, sniff something out.*

There are many idioms that are American in origin. Examples include:

to ride the gravy train (to do well financially without much work)
to raise the roof (to be enraged)
to paint the town red (to celebrate wildly)
to fly off the handle (to become abruptly angry)
a tough act to follow (to follow a stellar performance)
that hits the spot (that is just what was needed)
from the word "go" (from the beginning)
to act your age (to not act in an immature way)
pass the buck (to blame someone else)

head and shoulders above (to excel beyond others)
to do an about-face (to reverse one's position)

More studies of idiom comprehension have been conducted than those of any other figurative-language category. Maria Chiara Levorato and Christina Cacciari point out that older children comprehend more idioms than younger children, but the period between ages 7 and 11 (approximately second through sixth grade) is when idioms are learned most rapidly. These researchers have also found that it is more difficult for young learners to produce idiomatic expressions than to comprehend them.[9] Understanding idiomatic expressions and other nonliteral figures of speech is particularly troublesome for learners who do not speak English fluently or for whom English is not the first language. In 2005, according to Claude Goldenberg, 5 million students in the United States were classified as "an English-language learner (ELL), that is, a student who speaks English either not at all or with enough limitations that he or she cannot fully participate in mainstream English instruction.[10] " That is true of one of every nine students in our public schools. The majority of ELLs are Spanish speakers, but more than 400 language backgrounds (e.g., Cantonese, Vietnamese, Hmong, Arabic, Creole, Hindi) are native to students in our schools. Today's classroom teachers will find that many of their students, especially the English-language learners, need help with figurative language—idioms in particular. Idioms appear in all languages, and anyone who has tried to learn a second language knows that learning the idioms of a language is requisite for knowing that language.

Instructional Activity 6.1

Use context clues to infer the correct meaning for each underlined idiom in the following sentences. Answers are at the end of the chapter.

1. I have to crack the books before the test.
2. Spending all your money on candy is money down the drain.

3. I am not a good baseball player, so I spent all summer <u>warming the bench</u>.
4. Ms. Islip likes to give speeches because the audience <u>hangs on her every word</u>.
5. Jerry was <u>fishing for a compliment</u> when he showed me his hook shot.
6. Maura finally <u>came out of her shell</u> and started to enjoy her classmates.
7. After the local restaurant closed, Mr. Hosely spent two weeks <u>pounding the pavement</u> until he came here.
8. Lin said that she would <u>drum up some money</u> for the fair.
9. Daniel was <u>on top of the world</u> after his team won the debate.
10. Ms. Peters <u>missed the boat</u> when she didn't take the job in Nebraska.
11. The deal was made <u>behind closed doors</u>.
12. Jo had few friends because she always tried to <u>steal the spotlight</u>.

6.1

Younger students enjoy drawing pictures that show the humorous literal meanings of the words in idioms.

Below are some idioms and their meanings. Independently or in small groups, write a short story or informational piece using, in appropriate ways, as many of the following idioms as would make sense.

Idiom	Meaning
his bark is worse than his bite	his words are stronger than his actions
catch forty winks	take a short nap
see the handwriting on the wall	know something is going to happen
get the ball rolling	get something started
make small talk	talk about unimportant things
draw a blank	fail to remember
burn the midnight oil	work until late at night
a stuffed shirt	a self-important person
shake in our boots	be very frightened

kicking up their heels	celebrating
a backseat driver	one who gives unwanted advice
see eye-to-eye	to agree
a drop in the bucket	a small amount, not worth much

Similes and Metaphors

Teachers who want to introduce their students to the idea of metaphor may follow the approach introduced by the ancient Roman rhetorician Quintilian.[11] They begin by introducing similes that are explicitly stated comparisons helped by the words *like* and *as* (e.g., *After the downpour my shoes felt like sponges. The weight lifter's muscles are as solid as granite.*). Teachers then demonstrate how simple similes can be written as more abstract metaphors (e.g., *After the downpour my shoes were sponges. The weight lifter's muscles are granite.*).

David Crystal has identified two major types of metaphors:[12]

Conventional metaphors are a part of our everyday understanding and are processed without effort such as *"to lose the thread of an argument."*

Poetic metaphors combine conventional metaphors for literary purposes, especially poetry. [An example is *"Autumn comes moistly, as frost, rain, snow vie for the leaves. . . ."*[13]

Analyzing Similes

By beginning with similes, learners can grasp the notion of comparing two persons or things on some characteristic. The use of *like* or *as* makes the comparison explicit and therefore understandable. The following pattern of simple, mostly familiar similes helps demonstrate the comparison:

Simile: *The cabin was as warm as toast.*
Comparison: *cabin, toast*

Below are additional examples of similes and their comparisons.

Simile: *Joe works like a horse.*
Comparison: *Joe, horse*

Simile: *Patty is a lifeguard because she swims like a fish.*
Comparison: *lifeguard, fish*

Simile: *His expression was as sour as a lemon.*
Comparison: *expression, lemon*

Simile: *That hang glider soared like an eagle.*
Comparison: *hang glider, eagle*

Simile: *My grandfather is built like a pro football player.*
Comparison: *grandfather, pro football player*

Simile: *That bread is as dry as dust.*
Comparison: *bread, dust*

Simile: *The bank was as busy as a shopping mall on a Saturday.*
Comparison: *bank, shopping mall*

Simile: *Dr. Diller was as mad as a hornet.*
Comparison: *Dr. Diller, hornet*

Simile: *Our new student must feel like a fish out of water.*
Comparison: *new student, dry fish*

Simile: *My friendship with Bernice was as comfortable as an old shoe.*
Comparison: *friendship, broken-in shoe*

Instructional Activity **6.2**

Common similes (e.g., *as cold as ice, as warm as toast*) have a reputation for being trite—overused and stale. Create your own similes to complete the following sentences. Try to avoid comparisons that are worn-out and dull.

1. The house was as quiet as _____.
2. Emily tore down the display like _____.
3. The cold weather has been like _____.
4. She jumped the high hurdles as gracefully as _____.
5. That housefly flew into the garage like _____.
6. The light was as bright as _____.
7. At the start of school, the students were as happy as

 _____.
8. My uncle's new car is like _____.
9. The math lesson was like _____.
10. The path to the woods was as straight as _____.

6.2

Is the Well-Known Simile True?

Some common similes appear to be factual because they have been in use for so long. Owls have been associated with wisdom since ancient Greece; hence the simile *as wise as an owl.* But is an owl wiser than other birds? In fact, despite the owl's exceptional nocturnal vision, no data suggest that an owl is smarter than most other feathered friends.[14] The owl's large eyes probably make it appear studious, and some cartoonists have depicted the bird as wearing big eyeglasses to further emphasize the notion of wisdom.

Pigs have a reputation for being messy and not too particular about what they consume; therefore, the simile *eats like a pig* is not a flattering one. As Christine Ammer points out, however, pigs are actually smart and clean (they roll in mud to stay cool) and have remarkable digestive systems that allow them to eat just about anything.[15] When they are destined "to go to market," the humans who feed them want to add to their weight. So pigs, if they do overeat, are victims of circumstance.

In a 1966 study, Jim Anton delivered the rather surprising news that most birds don't sing, and those that do are mostly male; therefore, the simile *sings like a bird* should be used more selectively.[16] Some birdsongs are territorial warnings that have no pleasant intentions behind them.

On the other hand, *as cool as a cucumber* (i.e., relaxed and composed) is based on fact. As Irena Chalmers notes, the cucumber "literally maintains its insides at a temperature several degrees cooler than the surrounding atmosphere."[17] *Like rats off a sinking ship* has been in use for hundreds of years. Rats lived deep within sailing vessels. When ships started to leak, the lowest parts were flooded first. If sailors saw rats leaving their ship, it was a warning that the ship had a likely chance of going under.

Instructional Activity 6.3

Investigate the truth of the following common similes:
   eats like a bird, as hungry as a bear, memory like an elephant, and *as sly as a fox.*

6.3

Interpreting Metaphors

A metaphor is a figure of speech that compares two usually different things. Unlike similes, metaphoric comparisons are implicit, and the words *as* and *like* are not used. *The jump rope was a coiled snake* means that the jump rope was wound into spirals that gave it the appearance of a snake. When working with students, have them read sentences that contain metaphors and then write interpretations of the sentences. Here are some metaphors for your students:

New York City is an anthill.
The hurricane was a thousand voices screaming.
After the stores close, the parking lot is a desert.

Jeremy served concrete biscuits.

My cousin, Carmen, is a volcano.

Martha is an octopus when she wants to prevent an opponent from making a shot.

From the air the city is a quilt.

The distant lightning bolt was a flaming sword in the sky.

Nancy's attic is a museum.

Kennedy Airport is a welcome mat for the world.

Creating Metaphors

In pairs, create an original metaphor for each of the topics below.

tacos
his headache
the yellow bus
the musicians in the park
the new library
today's sunrise
her hands on the computer keyboard
our planet Earth
a city at night
the fast-food restaurant
Chi-ling's new sweater
the first warm day
spaghetti
that trash can
a cactus

Personification

David Crystal defines personification as

a type of metaphor in which human qualities are ascribed to nonhuman entities or notions. This kind of figurative expression is common in poetry (e.g., *The mountains spoke of ancient wars*), but there are many everyday examples (e.g., *The town slept*).[18]

Personification has been considered a unique figure of speech but also " . . . as an aspect of metaphor in which non-human is identified with human: 'Life can play some nasty tricks.'"[19] Although personification usually is found in poetry and literary writing, Tom McArthur points out such every-day uses of it as *Mother Nature, the mother of invention,* and *Father Time.*[20]

Instructional Activity   6.4

This activity features a task called "Personification Completion."
  Personification attaches human qualities to an animal, thing, or idea as seen in this example: *At dawn, the sleepy moon handed the sky over to the eager sun.* The moon and the sun are personified. They are given the human qualities of being tired or eager as well as the capacity to hand something over. Read the partial sentences below. Then choose a word or phrase from the list that follows to complete each example of personification. Answers are at the end of the chapter.

  1. _____ ate everything in its path.
  2. _____ slithered slowly on the busy highway.
  3. _____ felt relief when they finally jumped off.
  4. _____ raced from one person to the next.
  5. _____ cried out for company.
  6. _____ rose on cold, wet feet.
  7. _____ danced wildly in the storm.
  8. _____ seized hats and stole papers.
  9. _____ crept in and turned out the lights.
  10. _____ demanded her attention and insisted that she hurry.

The tree leaves	The forest fire	The gusty wind	Morning
The deserted beach	Darkness	Gossip	Heavy traffic
The trampoline	The doorbell		

Instructional Activity 6.5

In this activity, you are asked to "Write Your Own Personification."

Read the topics below. Think of potential human qualities for each topic and write a sentence for each topic that incorporates personification.

1. The sandwich
2. Our garbage bag
3. Telescopes
4. The condemned building
5. Traffic signals

6. A broken window
7. Balloons
8. The old photograph
9. Our crowded apartment
10. The tornado

6.5

Euphemisms

Euphemisms are vague or indirect expressions in which words are intentionally selected to evade certain other words that are thought to be too direct, negative, or offensive. Euphemistic words may be considered mild synonyms or even comforting synonyms. When we say *Juan's grandfather recently passed* or *Juan recently lost his grandfather*, we are using two euphemisms, *passed* and *lost*, as replacements for the more direct word *died*. The euphemistic *slender* and *trim* sound healthier than the unflattering adjectives *scrawny* and *skinny*. Examples of other common euphemistic words include:

Euphemism	Word or Words Replaced
accumulate	horde
disingenuous	lying
cash-flow difficulty	no money
downsize	fire people
food insecure	hungry
harvesting	hunting animals
inactive	lazy

inflexible	stubborn
lived-in	messy
message	television commercial
pests	cockroaches, rats, etc.
previously owned	used
unsuccessful attempt	failure

English-language speakers often seek ways of saying things to avoid sounding disrespectful, crude, uncaring, or obnoxious. New words continue to be coined, and old words are given new meanings in the continuing search for appropriate euphemisms.

Instructional Activity 6.6

Here the task is to "Replace the Euphemism."

Read each euphemism and write the word or words that the euphemism replaces. Suggested answers are at the end of the chapter.

1. inexpensive
2. fib
3. negative saver
4. bend the rules
5. medical procedure
6. career transition
7. landfill
8. conflict
9. suggested donation
10. ecotourism

6.6

Hyperbole

Hyperbole is intentional exaggeration that speakers and writers use to make a point or to emphasize an idea. *Ms. Zernick expects us to read about a thousand books a week* is an example of hyperbole. It means that Ms. Zernick assigns a lot of reading. Hyperbolic statements are not meant to be taken literally by the listener or reader. Hyperbole is sometimes found in literature, but it is more often used in everyday conversation. Here are some examples of sentences with hyperbole.

> She can hold her breath longer than a whale.
> The director told us that we were the best marching band in the universe.
> The lecture was so boring, it put me to sleep for a month.

Instructional Activity 6.7

This activity provides an opportunity to "create your own hyperbole." Read each topic and complete the sentence using original hyperbole.

1. The pizza delivery person
2. That new car
3. A bowl of soup at my aunt's house
4. Baseball doubleheaders
5. These mosquitoes
6. The temperature
7. Our lunchroom
8. Pat's suitcase
9. The Web site
10. The doctor's waiting room

6.7

Chiasmus

Language experts list *chiasmus* (kee-AZ-mus) as a type of figurative language.[21] Chiasmus consists of sentences or phrases in which the order of some of the words in the first sentence or phrase is reversed in the sentences or phrases that follow. For example, Thomas H. Huxley said, "Try to learn something about everything and everything about something." As Mardy Grothe notes, chiasmus

is as old as recorded civilization. It shows up in ancient Sanskrit, Mesopotamian, and Egyptian texts. It appears in ancient Chinese writings, including the *Analects* of Confucius. It was an integral feature of ancient Hebrew poetry and is common in both the Old and New Testaments.[22]

Perhaps the best-known chiasmus is the one in John F. Kennedy's inaugural address of January 20, 1961: "My fellow Americans: ask not what your country can do for you—ask what you can do for your country." President Barack Obama, in his election victory speech on November 6, 2008, also used chiasmus when he said, "My job is not to represent Washington to you but to represent you to Washington." Can you think of other examples of chiasmus?

Other Figures of Speech

Tom McArthur has identified various other types of figures of speech in his description of the topic.[23] They include *irony, litote, meiosis, oxymoron, synecdoche,* and more. *Irony* is a statement that is just the opposite of what is meant (e.g., *What a perfect time for this computer to break down* means that there couldn't be a worse time). A *litote* (LIE-tote) is an ironic understatement that uses a negative (e.g., *That wasn't a bad play* means that the play was rather good). *Meiosis* (my-OH-sis) is an intentionally belittling statement that strives to dismiss the significance of something (e.g., *That concert trombonist is a horn honker*). An *oxymoron* is a deliberate pairing of two words with contradictory intents (e.g., *with deliberate haste*). A *synecdoche* (si-NECK-da-key) is an expression in which a part of something is used to refer to the whole thing (e.g., *How do you like your new wheels?* when referring to a new car). A *synecdoche* also can be an expression in which the whole refers to the part (e.g., *In the summer*

Olympics, Japan trounced Norway for the gold, in which two countries refer to two teams).

Writers and speakers have a vast array of figurative-language devices from which to create colorful expressions rich in subtlety and imagination. Readers and listeners need to learn about these devices to fully understand and appreciate the language they encounter.

Answers to Instructional Activity 6.1

1. study hard	2. wasted
3. not allowed to play	4. listens intently
5. looking for praise	6. became less shy
7. looking for a job	8. earn or find money
9. feeling very good	10. missed an opportunity
11. in secret	12. get the attention

Answers to Instructional Activity 6.4

1. The forest fire	2. Heavy traffic
3. The trampoline	4. Gossip
5. The deserted beach	6. Morning
7. The tree leaves	8. The gusty wind
9. Darkness	10. The doorbell

Answers to Instructional Activity 6.6

1. cheap	2. lie
3. broke	4. cheat
5. surgical operation	6. unemployed
7. dump	8. war
9. entrance fee	10. camping

Notes

1. Bonnie von Hoff Johnson and Dale D. Johnson, "You're a Sage, Rosemary," *Proteus: A Journal of Ideas* 17, no. 1 (Spring 2000): 72. Used with permission from *Proteus: A Journal of Ideas*, themed issue on *Food*, Spring, 2000.

2. David Crystal, *A Dictionary of Language*, 2nd ed. (Chicago: University of Chicago Press, 1999), p. 116.

3. Theodore L. Harris and Richard E. Hodges, eds., *The Literacy Dictionary* (Newark, DE: International Reading Association, 1995), p. 84.

4. Tom McArthur, *The Concise Oxford Companion to the English Language* (Oxford, UK: Oxford University Press, 1996), p. 368.

5. Anthony Ortony, "Understanding Figurative Language," in *Handbook of Reading Research*, eds. P. David Pearson, Rebecca Barr, Michael Kamil, and Peter Mosenthal, 453–470 (New York: Longman, 1984), p. 467.

6. Christine Ammer, *Have a Nice Day—No Problem! A Dictionary of Clichés* (New York: Plume, 1992); Bonnie Johnson, *Wordworks: Exploring Language Play* (Golden, CO: Fulcrum Publishing, 1999).

7. Olivia A. Isil, *When a Loose Cannon Flogs a Dead Horse There's the Devil to Pay: Seafaring Words in Everyday Speech* (Camden, ME: International Marine, 1996), p. 59.

8. Johnson, *Wordworks*, p. 54.

9. Maria Chiara Levorato and Christina Cacciari, "The Effects of Different Tasks on the Comprehension and Production of Idioms in Children," *Journal of Experimental Child Psychology* 60 (1995): 261–283.

10. Claude Goldenberg, "Teaching English Language Learners: What the Research Does—and Does Not Say," *American Educator* 32, no. 2 (2008): 10.

11. McArthur, *The Concise Oxford Companion to the English Language*.

12. Crystal, *A Dictionary of Language*, p. 215.

13. Judie L. Strouf, *The Literature Teacher's Book of Lists* (West Nyack, NY: Center for Applied Research in Education, 1993), p. 166.

14. Jim Anton, *Wise Wacky Proverbs: The Truth Behind Everyday Sayings* (New York: Sterling, 1996).

15. Christine Ammer, *Cool Cats, Top Dogs, and Other Beastly Expressions* (Boston: Houghton Mifflin, 1999).

16. Anton, *Wise Wacky Proverbs*.

17. Irena Chalmers, *The Great Food Almanac* (San Francisco: Collins, 1994), p. 124.

18. Crystal, *A Dictionary of Language*, p. 257.

19. McArthur, *The Concise Oxford Companion to the English Language*, p. 684.

20. Ibid.

21. Ibid.; Crystal, *A Dictionary of Language*.

22. Mardy Grothe, *Never Let a Fool Kiss You or a Kiss Fool You: Chiasmus and a World of Quotations That Say What They Mean and Mean What They Say* (New York: Viking, 1999), p. x.

23. McArthur, *The Concise Oxford Companion to the English Language*.

7

Proverbs

Short Sentences Drawn from Long Experiences[1]

What words come to mind to complete these sentences?

Absence makes the heart _____.
You can't judge a book by _____.
There's no such thing as a free _____.
It's no use crying _____.
Don't put all your eggs _____.
Never put off until tomorrow what you _____.
Look before you _____.
Money doesn't grow _____.
You can't have your cake and _____.
All's well that ends _____.

The correct answers are *grow fonder, its cover, lunch, over spilled milk, in one basket, can do today, leap, on trees, eat it too,* and *well.* When completed correctly, all of the sentences above are proverbs. A *proverb* is a saying that provides advice or offers a thought about life. Proverbs have endured because they reflect common human experiences and wisdom.

The Importance of Proverbs

Some proverbs might remind us of times when we viewed a situation and uttered a pithy saying, or of times when we received unsolicited opinions from others. Perhaps you heard a proverb while being gently nagged "for your own good" by a parent or a guardian. Proverbs also serve a much broader, global purpose. As Wolfgang Mieder notes:

> In modern business and politics the understanding of proverbs plays a major role, often being the key to the success or breakdown of communications. It is a known fact that interpreters at the United Nations prepare themselves for their extremely sensitive job by learning proverbs of the foreign languages, since politicians often argue or attempt to convince their opponents by the use of a native proverb.[2]

Proverbs—with a word or few altered—frequently are used in advertising. Ad writers know that every word counts, and proverbs offer succinct and familiar ways to lure readers and listeners into a commercial message:

> Proverbs are used because their familiar sound creates a feeling of positive identification and trustworthy authority. . . . [C]opy writers have drawn heavily on proverbs to create slogans. By altering an existing proverb the memorability of the new slogan is literally assured.[3]

An example used by the car manufacturer Volkswagen—*Different Volks for different folks*[4]—is based on the African-American proverb *Different strokes for different folks*, which can be traced to the 1950s.[5]

The skeletons of proverbs also are used in headlines. For example, *The pen is mightier than the sword* can be traced to 1571,[6] but centuries later this familiar format was used in the *New York Times* arts-section headline "Greasepaint Can Be Mightier Than Pen or Sword" (October 15, 2008, p. C1). The *New York Times* business-section headline "With Banks Feeling the Heat, One in South Carolina Goes to the Kitchen" (November 12, 2008, p. B5) was based on the American proverb *If you can't stand the heat, get out of the kitchen,* used by President Harry Truman in 1952. And in *AM New York* (November 12, 2008, p. 16), an article about book-jacket design used the headline "Judging Books by Their Covers," based on the proverb *You can't judge a book by its cover.*

Proverbs add richness to language, and perhaps that is why so many great authors and orators (e.g., Cicero, Shakespeare, Dickens, Carl Sandburg, and Dr. Martin Luther King Jr.) used proverbs in their writing and speaking. Benjamin Franklin, known for his wit and wisdom, collected proverbs and included them in his *Poor Richard's Almanack*. Franklin is credited with Americanizing some proverbs. As Louis Berman notes, "A hands-on printer, Franklin shortened proverbs, perhaps to save typesetting time. Thus, 'He that goes a-borrowing goes a-sorrowing' became 'Borrowing brings sorrowing.'"[7]

Characteristics of Proverbs

Numerous proverbs have been found to have commonalities among them.[8] For instance, many proverbs are surprisingly old. They are concise and often rhyme. Some repeat sounds or words; others have more than the obvious meaning. Most deal with familiar topics and universal truths.

Ages of Some Proverbs

Several familiar proverbs and their dates of origin are listed below. Some of the words may differ from those we use today, because the proverbs were in use before American English was established—but the message is the same. Proverbs included in the "Complete the Sentences" exercise at the beginning of the chapter are marked with an asterisk (*). When the meanings of proverbs in this chapter are not obvious, they will be given in parentheses.

Proverb	Date of Origin
A good name is more valuable than money.	first century B.C.
Absence makes the heart grow fonder. (When people we care about are not near, we cherish them more.)	2 A.D.

Better late than never.   1330

*Look before you leap.   1350
   (Consider the facts before making a decision.)

Let sleeping dogs lie.   1385
   (Do not stir up trouble.)

*Never put off until tomorrow what you can do today.   1386

Out of sight, out of mind.   1450

*All's well that ends well.   1530
   (A happy ending erases earlier problems.)

If you want something done right, do it yourself.   1541

*You can't have your cake and eat it, too.   1546
   (You can't have everything that you want.)

Don't count your chickens before they're hatched.   1570
   (Do not count on something happening until
    it does.)

Live and learn.   1575

What you don't know can't hurt you.   1576

No news is good news.   1616

Great minds think alike.   1618

Live and let live.   1622

A penny saved is a penny earned.   1640
   (Saving money—no matter how little—is sensible.)

Necessity is the mother of invention.   1658
   (We discover or create things when we must.)

*It's no use crying over spilled milk.   1659
   (Do not worry about past problems.)

*Don't put all your eggs in one basket.   1662
   (Do not rely on just one person or thing.)

You can catch more flies with honey than with vinegar.   1666
   (It is better to treat people with kindness than
    with anger.)

It's never too late to learn.   1678

Don't bite the hand that feeds you.   1711
   (Be grateful to those who have helped you.)

Money doesn't grow on trees.	1750
(Money is earned—not found.)	
There's no such thing as a free lunch.	1840s
(People who give away things have expectations of the recipients.)	
You can't make an omelette without breaking some eggs.	1859
(A goal is not achieved without some difficulty.)	
Don't judge a book by its cover.	1929
(You cannot judge people or things by how they look.)	

Proverbs That Rhyme

Proverbs are passed from generation to generation, and some anthropologists study proverbs to understand a culture's members and what is of value to them.[9] In societies that relied on only oral communication—that is, societies without a writing system—proverbs had to be passed on through word of mouth. Perhaps that is one explanation as to why proverbs are short and many of them rhyme. The rhyming element serves as a memory aid just as rhyming elements in nursery rhymes help young children recall the rhymes. Here is a small sample of rhyming proverbs.

No pain, no gain. (Accomplishments require sacrifice.)

Haste makes waste. (Mistakes are caused by being in a hurry.)

Health is better than wealth.

What can't be cured must be endured.

Many strokes fell great oaks. (Small but steady actions can overcome big challenges.)

Two in distress make sorrow less. (Troubles are diminished when they are shared.)

No joy without annoy. (Happiness is not without some irritations, or others' happiness displeases some.)

Well begun is half done. (If you make a good start, the task will be simpler.)

East, west, home is best.

133

A friend in need is a friend indeed. (A good friend sticks with you when you are in trouble.)

It's always fair weather when friends get together. (Life seems better when we are with friends.)

Pay as you go, and nothing you'll owe. (Always use cash and you will not have debt.)

Birds of a feather flock together. (We are most comfortable with people who are like us.)

April showers bring May flowers. (What seems bad at the time can result in some good.)

Living in worry invites death in a hurry.

The sooner begun, the sooner done.

Loose lips sink ships. (Telling secrets can cause big problems.)

Early to bed, early to rise, makes one healthy, wealthy, and wise.

Life is hard by the yard, but by the inch life's a cinch. (Live life one day at a time.)

Little drops of water, little grains of sand, make a mighty ocean, and a pleasant land. (Impressive things are made of small elements.)

Proverbs That Repeat Sounds or Words

The repetition of sounds or words in proverbs engages listeners and also serves as a memory aid. Examples include:

Much coin, much care. (Money brings worry.)

They know most who know they know little. (Smart people know that there is much to learn.)

Never trouble trouble till trouble troubles you. (Do not look for problems unless they currently affect you.)

Willful waste brings woeful want. (If you waste things, you will end up with little.)

Where there's a will, there's a way. (Determination helps to achieve goals.)

Nothing ventured, nothing gained. (If you do not try to do something, you cannot accomplish it.)

Out of sight, out of mind. (When people are gone, we forget about them.)

If it looks like a duck, walks like a duck, and quacks like a duck, it's a duck. (Things are what they seem to be.)

Like likes like. (Similar people enjoy one another's company.)

Forgive and forget.

It's not over till it's over. (Do not give up until the end.)

First things first. (Prioritize tasks.)

Travel teaches tolerance. (Travel helps people understand different cultures.)

Never say never. (Conditions and people's minds change.)

Fight fire with fire. (Be just as aggressive as your opponent.)

Proverbs That Have More Than One Meaning

Many proverbs have meanings that go beyond their literal meanings. For example, *You can lead a horse to water, but you can't make it drink* literally means that a horse will drink water only if thirsty, whereas its metaphorical meaning is that you can try to help someone by offering a solution or suggestion but cannot force that person to take your advice.

Instructional Activity 7.1

Here are some more proverbs with more than one meaning. What are the metaphorical meanings of the proverbs? Suggested answers are at the end of the chapter.

1. *Don't burn your candle at both ends.*
2. *Still water runs deep.*
3. *A handsome shoe often pinches the foot.*
4. *A bird in the hand is worth two in the bush.*
5. *Don't jump from the frying pan into the fire.*
6. *A house without books is like a room without windows.*
7. *People who live in glass houses shouldn't throw stones.*

8. *You can't put a square peg in a round hole.*
9. *The grass is always greener on the other side of the fence.*
10. *Don't put the cart before the horse.*

Contradictory Proverbs

As Louis Berman has observed:

> In the world of practical affairs, we are accustomed to living with contradictions of all sorts. We blow on our hands to warm them up and blow on hot food to cool it off. A physician recommends that one patient eat less and that another eat more.[10]

Certain proverbs are contradictory, too—perhaps because people often alter their views or actions to accommodate life's circumstances. *Too many cooks spoil the broth* is an appropriate proverb when many opinions halt progress, but *Many hands make light work* is suitable when a large project requires the input of more than one person. Below are pairs of contradictory proverbs.

Haste makes waste.
Strike while the iron is hot. (Seize opportunities when they are available.)

Out of sight, out of mind.
Absence makes the heart grow fonder.

Better safe than sorry. (Caution is better than recklessness.)
Nothing ventured, nothing gained.

Slow help is no help.
Slow and steady wins the race.

The early bird catches the worm. (Early risers achieve more.)
Late is often lucky. (The last to arrive sometimes has an advantage.)

Those who hesitate are lost. (Do not ponder too long, or you will miss an opportunity.)
Look before you leap.

What you see is what you get. (People and things are what they seem to be.)
Appearances are deceiving. (People and things may not be what they seem to be.)

Quit while you're ahead.
A quitter never wins and a winner never quits.

Proverbs from Around the World

Every country has proverbs. Some proverbs from different countries have similar meanings. For example, *When the cat goes away, mice reign* (African, Swahili), *When the cat is gone, the mice come out to stretch themselves* (Chinese), and *When the cat's away, the mice will play* (English) mean that when there is no threat, people tend to act more freely. Other proverbs are unique to a country or region's geography or customs. Examples include:

Southern United States: *Don't call the alligator "big mouth" until you have crossed the river.* (Do not criticize someone unless you are secure.)

Egypt: *Cover up the good you do—do like the Nile and conceal your sources.* (Do not brag about your good deeds.)

Japan: *You should climb Mount Fujiyama once in your life. Climb it twice and you're a fool.* (You are foolish if you tackle a huge and possibly dangerous task more than once.)

Madagascar: *Cross the river among a crowd and the crocodile won't eat you.* (Things are safer when done with others.)

Here are some more proverbs from around the world.[11]

Turkey: *Everything is worn out with usage—except for experience.*

Netherlands: *With hard work, you can get fire out of a stone.* (You can accomplish the unimaginable with diligence and effort.)

France: *While the dogs are growling at each other, the wolf eats the sheep.* (When some people argue with each other, others will take advantage of the situation.)

Philippines: *Excessive courtesy can harm no one.*

Italy: *Good bargains empty the purse.* (You can spend too much by trying to save money.)

Mexico: *Though a cage may be made of gold, it is still a cage.* (No matter how comfortable it may seem, a lack of freedom is still restrictive.)

New Zealand, Maori: *Never spend time with people who don't respect you.*

Germany: *People show their character by what they laugh at.*

Japan: *Even when months and days are long, life is short.*

Denmark: *Bad is never good until worse happens.*

Peru: *You won't catch trout without wetting your feet.* (Accomplishments involve difficulties.)

Ireland: *Be happy with what you have and you will have plenty to be happy about.*

Jamaica: *The best passion is compassion.*

Africa, Zulu: *Even an ant can hurt an elephant.* (Even the "weak" can topple the powerful.)

Russia: *There is no proverb without a grain of truth.*

Instructional Activity 7.2

Find more proverbs from other lands and illustrate them on a poster for a class session on "Proverbs from Around the World."

7.2

Native American Proverbs

Native American ethnic groups used proverbs as a part of their oral tradition long before contact with European explorers. Guy Zona collected numerous Native American proverbs from "living orators of their local and national assemblies and tribal functions."[12] Among these proverbs are:

Crow: *One has to face fear or forever run from it.*
Hopi: *Do not allow anger to poison you.*
Arapaho: *Take only what you need and leave the land as you found it.*
Omaha: *He who is present at a wrongdoing and does not lift a hand to prevent it is as guilty as the wrongdoers.*

More American Proverbs

In addition to this wealth of Native American proverbs are many others that originated in the United States. As noted in *Wordworks*: "We are an inventive people who don't like to wallow in wordiness,"[13] and proverbs seem to fit our penchant for saying a lot in a few words. Below are proverbs that had their origin in the United States.[14]

Money doesn't grow on trees. (1750)
Oil and water don't mix. (1783) (People with opposing viewpoints do not get along well.)
The best defense is a good offense. (1795) (You might have to go on the attack to protect yourself.) [used by President George Washington]
An apple never falls far from the tree. (1839) (We are, in many ways, similar to our parents.)
Money isn't everything. (1842)
Talk is cheap. (1843) (Talk alone does not accomplish things.)
Don't bite off more than you can chew. (1886) (Do not take on more challenges than you can handle.)
Opposites attract. (1918)
Crime doesn't pay. (1927)

The best things in life are free. (1927) [A variation is *The best things in life aren't things.*]

Don't judge a book by its cover. (1929)

If you can't beat 'em, join 'em. (1941)

It's not what you know but who you know. (1945) (Some people get jobs because of connections—not talent.)

If anything can go wrong, it will. (1949)

It's not whether you win or lose but how you play the game. (1954)

When the going gets tough, the tough get going. (1956) [used by President John F. Kennedy's father]

A rising tide will lift all boats. (1960) (Prosperity is good for everyone.) [used by President John F. Kennedy]

Don't get mad, get even. (1965) (Revenge is better than anger.)

What goes around, comes around. (1970) (What you do to others may be done to you.)

It's not over till it's over. (1973) (Do not give up until the final results are determined.) [used by baseball legend Yogi Berra]

If is ain't (isn't) broke, don't fix it. (1977) (Do not try to improve on something that does not need improvement.)

Collections from the Fifty States

As J. R. Moehringer points out:

> Say what you want about fading regional differences, about the steam-rolling effects of mass culture, Americans still feel uniquely defined by whichever state they call home. That familiar, multicolored map hanging in every grade-school classroom is a periodic table, setting out the 50 basic elements of our national character. Squares, trapezoids, spherical blobs—the states may be arbitrary shapes drawn on the land, but somehow they shape us. They help determine how we talk, what we eat and the various ways we regard one another.[15]

A Dictionary of American Proverbs[16] exhibits the variety of proverbs used in each of the fifty states. The collection took forty years of field research to compile. Although not all of the proverbs in the *Dictionary* are American in origin, the proverbs were in use in specific states when they were recorded by those working on the project. Here are examples from some of the states.

Alabama: *Constant cheerfulness is a sign of true wisdom.* (A positive attitude shows intelligence.)

Arizona: *When fortune frowns, friends are few.* (False friends stay away when you are in trouble.)

Arkansas: *Friday begun, never done.* (You will not finish a task if you do not give it your best effort.)

California: *All the darkness in the world cannot put out a single candle.* (Negativity cannot diminish hope.)

Florida: *Envy is destroyed by true friendship.* (Friends are not jealous of one another.)

Illinois: *Courtesy costs nothing.*

Indiana: *Action is worry's worst enemy.* (Work eliminates worry.)

Iowa: *In this world, nothing is permanent except change.* (Nothing ever stays the same.)

Kansas: *Long faces make short lives.* (To stay healthy, stay happy.)

Kentucky: *Too much bed makes a dull head.* (Laziness does nothing for the intellect.)

Louisiana: *To know everything is to know nothing.* (People who think that they know a lot often do not.)

Maryland: *Common sense is the rarest thing in the world and the most valuable.*

Michigan: *Constant complaints never get pity.*

Minnesota: *It is easier to give advice than to take it.*

Mississippi: *You can't have the ear unless you plant the corn.* (You cannot get a reward unless you work for it.)

Nebraska: *Always tell your doctor and your lawyer the truth.*

New Jersey: *Those who think they can't generally are right.* (People with a poor self-concept often do not succeed.)

New Mexico: *The best place for criticism is in front of your mirror.* (Do not criticize others until you have examined your own life.)

New York: *There are a lot of bumps in the road to Easy Street.* (It is not simple to accomplish a lot.)

North Carolina: *Take advantage of the little opportunities, and you won't need to wait for the big one.*

North Dakota: *Not even a schoolteacher notices bad grammar in a compliment.*

Ohio: *Somewhere behind the clouds the sun is shining.* (Difficult times may hide the good that is happening.)

Oklahoma: *A clean conscience is a good pillow.* (People who do not do bad things sleep better.)

Oregon: *Freedom comes before silver and gold.* (Freedom is more important than riches.)

Rhode Island: *A bad day never has a good night.*

South Carolina: *To be content, look backward on those who possess less than yourself, not forward on those who possess more.*

Tennessee: *The good old days were once the present, too.* (As time passes, we tend to forget the bad things that have happened.)

Texas: *Many drops of water will sink a ship.* (Nitpicking can destroy big ideas.)

Utah: *Never find your delight in another's misfortune.*

Vermont: *Don't complain about the boat that carries you over safely.* (Be grateful to those who have helped you.)

Wisconsin: *The only difference between stumbling blocks and stepping stones is the way you use them.* (Some people can look at difficulties as challenges.)

Proverbs in Pretentious English

Pretentious English is a writing style that uses difficult synonyms or related words in place of common words.

Instructional Activity 7.3

The following well-known proverbs are written in pretentious English. How many of them do you recognize? (Answers are at the end of the chapter.) As an additional activity, try to stump your classmates. Select several proverbs from this chapter and write them in pretentious English. How many can they decipher? *Tip:* An unabridged dictionary or large thesaurus can help you find appropriate synonyms and related words.

Example: Produce fodder during old sol's luminance.

Answer: *Make hay while the sun shines.*

1. Confabulation is penurious.
2. Veracity is the preeminent protocol.
3. Combat conflagration with combustion.
4. Specie does not propagate on partially hard, fibrous perennials.
5. Celerity forges profligacy.
6. A member of the class Aves is equivalent to a couple in the brier.
7. Disconsolateness relishes assemblage.
8. Allow somnolent members of the family Canidae repose.
9. Each cirrus and stratus has an Ag interior.
10. A scrutinized receptacle at no time effervesces.

7.3

Are These Proverbs Always True?

A picture is worth a thousand words is an American proverb first used in 1921 in the publication *Printers' Ink.*[17] Louis Berman has provided a quotation by Leo Rosten that counters that proverb: "Draw me a picture of the Gettysburg Address."[18] *Money can't buy happiness* is another American proverb—in this case, one that can be traced to 1792.[19] Money certainly can buy the best medical care, comfortable surroundings, and plenty to eat, but can it buy happiness? According to one researcher, when 500 respondents were asked if money would make them happy, the vast majority answered that all it would take was winning a lottery jackpot—for them, the best things in life were *not* free. However studies of state lottery winners have shown that most of them are made miserable by their windfalls. They overextend themselves with purchases, become the targets of greedy relatives and scam artists, are besieged by charities, and are ultimately let down by their own high expectations that money would buy them happiness.[20]

Instructional Activity 7.4

In small groups, discuss the following proverbs. Give real-life examples that support or refute the proverbs.

1. *One who slings mud loses ground.*
2. *An apple a day keeps the doctor away.*
3. *Feed a cold, starve a fever.*
4. *Don't start anything you can't finish.*
5. *Experience is the best teacher.*
6. *One of these days is none of these days.*
7. *Business before pleasure.*
8. *The customer is always right.*
9. *Misery loves company.*
10. *Where there's smoke, there's fire.*

7.4

Proverbs are words of wisdom from around the world. As noted in this chapter, some are ancient and others are relatively new. Some express acknowledged truths and others provide advice or share points of view. The richness of all cultures can be seen in their proverbs, and they often are found in our best writing and public speaking.

Suggested Answers to Instructional Activity 7.1

1. Do not work too hard.

2. Quiet people can hide underlying thoughts.
3. Some things that look good can harm one.
4. To have something certain is better than to wish for something more.
5. Do not go from a bad situation to one that is worse.
6. Knowledge opens the mind.
7. People who have flaws should not point out the flaws of others.
8. You cannot change the way people are.
9. We always think that some have it better than we do, but they do not.
10. Do things in the proper order.

Answers to Instructional Activity 7.3

1. *Talk is cheap.*
2. *Honesty is the best policy.*
3. *Fight fire with fire.*
4. *Money doesn't grow on trees.*
5. *Haste makes waste.*
6. *A bird in the hand is worth two in the bush.*
7. *Misery loves company.*
8. *Let sleeping dogs lie.*
9. *Every cloud has a silver lining.*
10. *A watched pot never boils.*

Notes

1. The subtitle of this chapter—"Short Sentences Drawn from Long Experiences"—is based on a quote by Miguel de Cervantes (1547–1616).

2. Wolfgang Mieder, *The Prentice-Hall Encyclopedia of World Proverbs* (New York: MJF Books, 1986), pp. x, xi.

3. Wolfgang Mieder and Barbara Mieder, "Tradition and Innovation: Proverbs in Advertising," in *Wisdom of Many: Essays on the Proverb*, ed. Wolfgang Mieder and Alan Dundes, 309–322 (Madison: University of Wisconsin Press, 1994), pp. 312, 313.

4. Ibid., p. 314.

5. Gregory Y. Titelman, *Popular Proverbs and Sayings* (New York: Gramercy Books, 1996); Martin H. Manser, *The Facts on File Dictionary of Proverbs* (New York: Checkmark Books, 2002).

6. Titelman, *Popular Proverbs and Sayings.*

7. Louis Berman, *Proverb Wit and Wisdom* (New York: Perigee, 1997), pp. xii, xiii.

8. Bonnie Johnson, *Wordworks: Exploring Language Play* (Golden, CO: Fulcrum Publishing, 1999).

9. Mieder, *The Prentice-Hall Encyclopedia of World Proverbs.*

10. Berman, *Proverb Wit and Wisdom*, p. xx.

11. Mieder, *The Prentice-Hall Encyclopedia of World Proverbs*; Gerd de Ley, *International Dictionary of Proverbs* (New York: Hippocrene Books, 1998); Johnson, *Wordworks.*

12. Guy Zona, *The Soul Would Have No Rainbow If the Eyes Had No Tears and Other Native American Proverbs* (New York: Touchstone, 1994), pp. 10, 16, 88, 115, 125.

13. Johnson, *Wordworks*, p. 108.

14. Wolfgang Mieder, Stewart A. Kingsbury, and Kelsie B. Harder, *A Dictionary of American Proverbs* (New York: Oxford University Press, 1992); Titelman, *Popular Proverbs and Sayings*; Johnson, *Wordworks*; Manser, *The Facts on File Dictionary of Proverbs.*

15. J. R. Moehringer, "Big Country," review of *State by State: A Panoramic Portrait of America*, eds. Matt Weiland and Sean Wilsey, *New York Times Book Review*, October 12, 2008, p. 14.

16. Mieder, Kingsbury, and Harder, *A Dictionary of American Proverbs*, pp. 6, 8, 10, 42, 59, 74, 81, 90, 94, 104, 107, 110, 112, 114, 117, 120, 127, 134, 135, 136, 143, 156, 169, 182, 185, 193, 230, 232, 233, 570.

17. Ibid., p. 463.

18. Quoted in Berman, *Proverb Wit and Wisdom*, p. 328.

19. Mieder, Kingsbury, and Harder, *A Dictionary of American Proverbs*, p. 416.

20. Charles Panati, *Words to Live By: The Origins of Conventional Wisdom and Commonsense Advice* (New York: Penguin Books, 1999), p. 121.

Onomastics

The World of Names

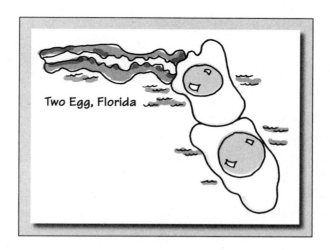

Two Egg, Florida

Would you rather be a resident of Skunk Waddle Apartments or of Flowering Meadows Residences?

Which is tastier: Monkey Stew or Stew à la Parisienne?

If you were relocating, which town would be more inviting—sight unseen: Roachville or Scenic Shores?

Would you eat in a restaurant called Grimy Corners in an unfamiliar city?

Names are so common, we tend to take them for granted without understanding their influence on our perceptions or purchasing habits. *Onomastics*, the study of names, rarely is addressed in school curricula even though students encounter names daily. Businesspeople, among other groups, are keenly aware of the importance of names. Some companies do nothing but create names for products and businesses. As Laura and Al Ries note in *The Fall of Advertising and the Rise of PR*, "Nothing in marketing can succeed unless the name is right. The best company, the best product, the best packaging, and the best marketing in the world won't work if the name is wrong."[1]

Some familiar edibles originally had what the Rieses refer to as "loser names."[2] They include *horse mackerel* (now called *tuna fish*), *gooseberries* (now called *kiwi fruit*), and *filberts* (now called *hazelnuts*). "Brand names can influence how food products taste to consumers,"[3] and so can menu descriptors. Brian Wansink found, for example, that when *Seafood Fillet* on a menu was renamed *Succulent Italian Seafood Fillet*, its sales jumped 27 percent even though the dish and price remained identical. Subjects in Wansink's research also reported that foods with more appealing names tasted better. "Traditional Cajun Red Beans with Rice" sold better and was rated as better tasting than "Red Beans and Rice" even though, just as with the seafood fillets, the dishes and prices were unchanged. In addition, Wansink found that sensory names (e.g., Velvety Cream Pudding, Sizzling Burgers), nostalgic names (e.g., Grandma's Homemade Pasta Shells), and geographic labels (e.g., Wisconsin Cheese Snackers) help to boost restaurant sales and increase diners' satisfaction.[4] Names are so crucial to food sales that some culinary schools offer future chefs lessons on how to write menus with attractive names for their dishes.[5]

In an earlier book, we compared school lunch menus from an underfunded Louisiana elementary school to menus from a private school in New York City where tuition per child was close to $30,000 per year. The school that served children of poverty listed "sausage," "tator [*sic*] tots," "corn," and "peas" among its menu items. The private school, where all of the chefs were graduates of the French Culinary Institute, included "quinoa with sautéed shiitakes," "roasted codfish with crisp panko and mustard top," and "brown basmati rice pilaf" among its menu items.[6]

Real estate developers also know the importance of names. As Bill Bryson points out, a name change "can give property values an instant boost of up to 15 percent."[7] Perhaps that is why residents on *Fink's Hideaway*, a pleasant thoroughfare in a north-central Louisiana city, recently changed its name to *Hideaway Road*. People in the entertainment world likewise change their names to something catchier or less complicated than their given names to make their personas more memorable or appealing to their audiences. Examples include Frances Gumm to Judy Garland, Marion Michael Morrison to John Wayne, Henry John Deutchendorf Jr., to John Denver, and Annie Mae Bullock to Tina Turner. Public relations executives advise job seekers to use wholesome-sounding names in their e-mail addresses—no PoohBear, Silly Lily, or Hunkster.[8]

There are several categories of names. *Anemonyms*, for example, are names of storms and winds. Hurricanes' names are chosen by the World Meteorological Organization. Names of especially destructive hurricanes, such as *Katrina*, *Hugo*, and *Gloria*, are never used again.

Odonyms are names of streets, such as *Maple Drive* and *Riverside Boulevard*. Paul Dickson notes three major periods of assigning names to American streets.[9] During the first of these, from 1682 to 1945, streets were given mostly numerical names (e.g., Second Street), tree names (e.g., Birch Lane), and names of well-known people (e.g., Jefferson Drive); some were named for businesses on those streets (e.g., Mill Road) or for the towns or cities to which the streets go (e.g., Chicago Street). From 1945 to 1960, a lot of peaceful words such as *Hollow*, *Forest*, and *Pond* were used in street names. And themes have been big during the third era, from 1960 to the present. An example is the author theme (Agatha Christie Lane, Thackeray Drive) found in a new subdivision near Green Bay, Wisconsin.

Pseudonyms are false names for people or places. *Pen names* are pseudonyms selected by writers to hide their real identity. Examples include Mark Twain for Samuel Langhorne Clemens and Pearl Buck for Pearl Comfort Sydenstricker. *Aptronyms* are names that are suited to people's profession. And as Silla Brush points out, "Since the late 1990s, *New Scientist* magazine has taken note of 'nominative determinism,' the phenomenon of people whose career choices could have been inspired by their surnames."[10] Brush gives several examples of aptronyms including Ernest B. Fish, who directs the Texas Tech Wildlife and Fisheries Management Institute, and David W. Music, a music professor at a southern university. In the remainder of this chapter, we focus on four other types of names: eponyms, toponyms, demonyms, and city and town names.

Eponyms

An *eponym* is a word named after a person or a figure in mythology. *Leotard* is an eponym. It is named after Jules Leotard (1842–1870), a circus performer who popularized the snug article of clothing. *Cereal* also is an eponym. In Roman mythology, *Ceres* was the goddess of agriculture.

Instructional Activity 8.1

In the list below, each word is followed by a brief statement of "origin." Some of the origins are true—they actually are eponyms. Other origins are false—we made them up. Which are the real eponyms? Answers are at the end of the chapter.

1. *barracuda:* This tropical fish with a rather frightening appearance and reputation was named for the Spanish scientist Álvaro Mateo Barracuda (1832–1889). Barracuda was known as a fearless pursuer of scientific knowledge. A statue honoring Barracuda's explorations can be found in Rio de Janeiro's Bartolomé Plaza.
2. *caboose:* The last car on some freight trains was named for William Myron Caboose (1819–1868). Caboose worked on the design of the first transcontinental railroad, a meeting of the Union and Central Pacific Railroads, but died a year short of its completion.
3. *diesel:* Rudolph Diesel was committed to designing a better engine after a tiring, several-day ride on a steam-powered train. Diesel's engines eventually found their way into trucks, trains, and other engine-propelled conveyances. Although Diesel became a wealthy man, he died a mysterious death in 1913 at the age of 55.
4. *gavel:* Sir Thomas Gavel, a British judge who lived from 1659 to 1726, is credited with devising this small hammer to use in his court of law. To this day, gavels are used to get a group's attention or restore order in a gathering.

5. *guppy:* This little fish, often found in aquariums, is named after R. J. Lechmere Guppy (1836–1916). Mr. Guppy lived in Trinidad, was a clergyman, and studied fish on the side. He discovered the small fish in 1850 and sent a sample of one to the British Museum in 1850.

6. *kilt:* This garment is named for Angus McKilt, a Scottish hero of the Middle Ages who defiantly wore it into battle as a sign of Scottish clan pride. McKilt was captured by the British and executed outside the Tower of London in 1272. The kilt is still worn in Scottish ceremonies.

7. *maverick:* Samuel Augustus Maverick (1803–1870) was a Texas lawyer and politician who owned a large ranch. He did not follow the custom of branding his cattle. In addition to unbranded cattle, the word now refers to someone with independent thoughts and actions.

8. *melba toast:* This dry, hard toast is named in honor of opera singer Dame Nellie Melba (1861–1931). Melba took her name from Melbourne, Australia. In stark contrast to the low-calorie toast, the rich dessert peach Melba also is named after her.

9. *newt:* Sir Reginald Charles Newt (1860–1911), a famed naturalist of his time, described this salamander-like amphibian in his journal while on one of several trips to Africa. The Royal Biological Society of London named the creature after him to honor his many scientific accomplishments.

10. *salmonella: Salmonella* was named for Daniel Elmer Salmon (1850–1914), a veterinarian who in 1885 discovered the bacterium that causes a type of food poisoning. Salmon's work was the impetus for our current meat-inspection program.

11. *saxophone:* This popular brass band instrument was patented by Adolphe Sax in 1835. Adolphe learned how to make musical instruments from his father, Charles Sax.

12. *tetrazzini:* Chicken or turkey tetrazzini, made with noodles, mushrooms, cheese, and other ingredients, was named by a French chef in honor of the Italian opera singer Luisa Tetrazzini (1871–1940).

8.1

There are tens of thousands of eponyms. The medical field alone lays claim to 18,000 of them.[11] *Parkinson's disease*, for example, is named for British physician James Parkinson (1755–1828) and *Down syndrome* is named for John Langdon Down (1828–1896), who also was a British physician.

Below are some well-known eponyms and a brief description for each.[12] If you or your students are interested in pursuing the study of eponyms, several eponym dictionaries are available in public libraries.

Achilles' heel, Achilles tendon   In Greek mythology, Achilles was a hero of the Trojan War. His heel was his weak spot because he was held by it when dipped into a river to protect his body from injury. Today, *Achilles' heel* refers to a person's vulnerability in some respect. The *Achilles tendon* connects the heel bone to the calf muscles.

Alzheimer's disease   This condition, characterized by loss of memory, was described by German neurologist Alois Alzheimer (1864–1915) as early as 1907.

ampere (amp)   This unit of electrical current was named for André Marie Ampère (1775–1836), a French physicist.

atlas   Atlas was a character in Greek mythology who, as a punishment for making war on Zeus, was made to hold up the heavens on his shoulders. In the 1500s, geographers began using a picture of Atlas on their map collections.

boycott   Captain Charles Boycott (1832–1897), an English land agent, was defied and ostracized by his Irish tenants when he tried to raise their rents after a dismal harvest. Boycott eventually had to leave Ireland because of their actions.

cardigan   The next time you see or wear a cardigan sweater, you might think of James Thomas Brudenell, Earl of Cardigan (1797–1863). He frequently wore a sweater that looks just like our version today. According to historians, although the earl was courageous in war, his disposition was so disagreeable that Londoners threw stones at him in public places.

Celsius The Celsius temperature scale, on which water freezes at 0 degrees and boils at 100 degrees, was created by Anders Celsius (1701–1744), a Swedish astronomy professor just like his father.

Doberman pinscher German Ludwig Dobermann was, among other things, a tax collector. It is not difficult to figure out why he bred this protective dog in the late 1800s.

Douglas fir (or spruce) David Douglas (1798–1834) was a Scottish botanist who "discovered" these huge trees while exploring the American wilderness in 1825. Douglas lived to be only 36 years old; he was killed by a wild bull while exploring in Hawaii.

Fahrenheit Gabriel Daniel Fahrenheit (1686–1736) was an orphan by the age of 15. Despite his lack of formal education, he invented the thermometer and set a scale of 32 degrees for the freezing of water and 212 degrees for the boiling of water.

Ferris wheel This popular amusement-park ride was designed and built by George W. G. Ferris of Illinois. Ferris's wheel was the hit of Chicago's World Columbian Exposition in 1893.

Gallup poll Iowan George Horace Gallup (1901–1984) was a journalism professor who began his polling career by conducting surveys for newspapers.

gardenia Known for its heavy scent, white flowers, and waxy, deep-green leaves, this shrub is a native of Africa and Asia. It is named after Alexander Garden (1730–1791), a South Carolina physician who also was a well-known botanist.

Jacuzzi Candido Jacuzzi (1903–1986) was born in Italy and immigrated to America. He was an engineer who manufactured hydraulic pumps. Jacuzzi designed a specific pump for use in a tub to ease the pain experienced by his child, who suffered from rheumatoid arthritis. From this design, the Jacuzzi was born.

Oscars Prior to 1931, there was no name for the statuette presented to members of the movie industry by the Academy of Motion Picture Arts and Sciences at their annual gathering. Oscar got his name when the Academy's librarian, Margaret Herrick, said that it looked like her uncle, Oscar Pierce.

ritzy   This adjective, meaning "expensive and elegant," comes from César Ritz (1850–1918), who managed and owned a series of luxurious European hotels bearing his surname.

Sequoia   Giant redwoods, the tallest trees in the world, are named for Sequoyah (1776–1843), a Cherokee chief's grandson. After twelve years of arduous intellectual work, he completed a written Cherokee language.

silhouette   Etienne de Silhouette (1709–1767) was a French finance minister who was known as a penny pincher. Anything sparse or cheap was referred to as a *silhouette*—including black cutouts of figures for those who could not afford more elaborate portraits.

Tony awards   These awards are presented annually for theatrical accomplishments. Broadway productions that win a Tony usually can count on increased box-office sales. The silver medallions are named for Antoinette "Tony" Perry (1888–1946), who was the founder of the American Theater Wing.

Venn diagram   This visual, which consists of two overlapping circles to illustrate shared and unique features when making comparisons, was named after Englishman John Venn (1834–1923), a teacher of logic.

Instructional Activity 8.2

Caesar salad and *fettuccine Alfredo* are food eponyms. *Caesar salad* was created by Tijuana, Mexico, restaurateur Caesar Cardini between the 1920s and 1930s, and *fettuccine Alfredo* was a 1920s creation of Roman chef Alfredo di Lellio. Use an eponym dictionary or the Internet to find the origins of the following food eponyms:

beef Stroganoff	*eggs Benedict*
beef Wellington	*Graham crackers*
chateaubriand	*oysters Rockefeller*
Cobb salad	*sandwich*

8.2

Toponyms

A *toponym* is a word named after a real or imaginary place. *Hamburger*, for example, is a toponym. It is named after the city of Hamburg, Germany. *Shangri-la* refers to a paradise-like setting. This toponym comes from an imaginary place in the British novel *Lost Horizon*. Below are just a few common toponyms.[13]

canary   This little yellow finch is named after the Canary Islands, which are located just off the northwest coast of Africa.

cologne   Cologne, a scent lighter than perfume, was first produced in Cologne, Germany (the German *Köln*).

frankfurter   This sausage is named after Frankfurt am Main, Germany.

limousine   The Limousin area of France is the referent for this word.

magenta   This color got its name from the blood that was spilled at the Battle of Magenta, Italy, in 1859. A purplish-pink dye from coal was discovered soon after the battle and was given the name *magenta*.

paisley   Paisley, Scotland, is the home of this swirling, usually colorful pattern.

sardine   The name of this small, tasty fish comes from Sardinia, an Italian island in the Mediterranean Sea.

tuxedo   This familiar article of formal wear is named after Tuxedo Park, New York, where a wealthy resident popularized the fashion in 1886.

Instructional Activity   8.3

The following cheeses are toponyms:

Cheddar, Colby, Edam, Emmental, Gorgonzola, Gruyère, Parmesan, Roquefort, Stilton.

From which locales did their names originate? (Answers are at the end of the chapter.) Do you know any other words that are toponyms?

8.3

Demonyms

A *demonym* is the name for a person who lives in a particular place. We live in Manhattan, a borough of New York City, so we are Manhattanites and New Yorkers. Although there are lists of rules on how to create demonyms, research reveals that "people in a place tend to decide what they will call themselves, whether they be *Angelenos* (from Los Angeles) or *Haligonians* (from Halifax, Nova Scotia)."[14] Some demonyms, such as *Bostonian*, are simple to decipher, but others, including several in the list below, can present challenges even to competent readers.[15]

Place Name	Demonym
Annapolis (Maryland)	Annapolitan
Asbury Park (New Jersey)	Asbury Parker
Bern (Switzerland)	Bernese
Cape Cod	Cape Codder
Cedar Falls (Iowa)	Cedar Fallsan
Delaware	Delawarean
Dijon (France)	Dijonese
Florida	Floridian
Glasgow (Scotland)	Glaswegian
Liverpool (England)	Liverpudlian
Maine	Mainer
Naples (Italy)	Neapolitan
Nashville	Nashvillian
Taos (New Mexico)	Taoseno
Wichita Falls (Texas)	Wichitan

Instructional Activity **8.4**

Find demonyms for ten towns and cities in your state. Try to include some demonyms that are not apparent.

8.4

City and Town Names

There are onomasticians who believe that *nicknames* are older than *surnames* (i.e., people's last names). Nicknames such as *Tiny* and *Big Head* have been found on ancient Egyptian artifacts.[16] Many cities and states also have nicknames, and these can cause comprehension difficulties if the reader or listener is not acquainted with them.

Instructional Activity 8.5

Can you match the following cities to their nicknames? Answers are at the end of the chapter.

City	Nicknames
1. Denver	A. The Big Easy
2. Detroit	B. Gateway to the West
3. Hollywood (California)	C. Steel City
4. International Falls (Minnesota)	D. The Mile High City
5. Los Angeles	E. Motor City
6. New Orleans	F. Tinseltown
7. Pittsburgh (Pennsylvania)	G. The Nation's Refrigerator
8. St. Louis	H. The City of Angels

Chicago's nickname is *The Windy City.* It is not the city's wind speeds that gave Chicago its nickname. Rather, as Michael Shook points out, the nickname came from Chicago's "long-winded" politicians. Chicago ranks sixteenth among windy cities; Great Falls, Montana is the windiest.[17]

With a partner, find the origins of the following city nicknames:

1. New York City, New York: The Big Apple
2. Boston, Massachusetts: The Athens of America
3. Philadelphia, Pennsylvania: The City of Brotherly Love
4. Dayton, Ohio: The Birthplace of Aviation
5. Seattle, Washington: The Emerald City

8.5

Instructional Activity 8.6

States have nicknames, too—and some have more than one nickname.[18] In the list below, can you match the explanation for the nickname with the correct state? Answers are at the end of the chapter.

1. In the 1800s, lead miners burrowed into caves that resembled badger homes. The nickname for this state is the *Badger State*.

   A. Indiana

2. In 1889, the government opened a large territory to settlers. The rush for land caused some pioneers to head for the territory before its official opening. They wanted to arrive sooner rather than later. The state's nickname is the *Sooner State*.

   B. Kansas

3. One reason this state is nicknamed the *Tar Heel State* is that tar was once a major product there. Another is that during the Civil War, its soldiers held their ground in battle as if they had tar on their heels.

   C. New Jersey

4. This state's nickname is the *First State* because it was the first to ratify the U.S. Constitution in 1787.

   D. Ohio

5. There are many theories about the origin of the nickname the *Hoosier State*. Some historians think that it was named for Mr. Sam Hoosier, who built canals in the state. Others think that it referred to pioneers, called *hoozers*, meaning "those living on high ground."

   E. Wisconsin

6. This state's nickname, the *Bay State*, refers to an early colony on a bay. The

   F. Delaware

demonym *Bay Staters* is certainly easier to
pronounce than the state's name plus a suffix.

7. The *Garden State* provides a lot of people   G. Oklahoma
   with fresh produce.

8. Women in this state were voting in 1869—   H. Massachusetts
   long before the Nineteenth Amendment in
   1920. The state's nickname, therefore,
   is the *Equality State.*

9. The *Buckeye State* gets its nickname from the   I. North Carolina
   state's many buckeye trees, whose fruit has
   the appearance of deer's eyes.

10. There are so many of these cheerful blooms   J. Wyoming
    in this state that its nickname is the
    Sunflower State.

8.6

Instructional Activity   8.7

Below are several other states nicknames. With a partner, identify the
states and the stories behind their nicknames.

1. the Yellowhammer State
2. the Centennial State
3. the Show Me State
4. the Magnolia State
5. the Silver State
6. the Granite State
7. the Green Mountain State
8. the Pelican State
9. the Old Line State
10. the Volunteer State

8.7

As American writer and philosopher Henry David Thoreau (1817–1862) wisely stated, "With knowledge of the name comes a distincter recognition and knowledge of the thing."[19] Knowing the history of some city and town names can provide an enjoyable way to integrate reading, geography, and history. For example, one small town in Scotland had to change its name because too many tourists were stealing the town's name sign. A town member said, "The longest any sign has lasted was three months, and one vanished after a day."[20] The town's name was *Lost* (Celtic for *inn*) before frustrated residents changed it to *Lost Farm.*

America has many colorful town names, too. For example, there is Bill, Montana. Bill got its name when a local woman noticed that there were a lot of men named Bill in town.[21] Transylvania, a small Louisiana town with a picture of a large bat on its water tower, was named by a person in the area who had ancestors from the Romanian province of Transylvania.[22] Nine Times, South Carolina, got is name because of a road that crossed a stream in the area nine times. Snowflake, Arizona, was named for Mr. Snow and Mr. Flake, two original residents of the town. In a village in Tennessee, a store owner prefaced every price with "only," and that is how Only, Tennessee, got its name.[23]

Instructional Activity 8.8

In a small group, find the stories behind five of the following towns.

1. Eighty-four, Pennsylvania
2. Siren, Wisconsin
3. Peculiar, Missouri
4. Two Egg, Florida
5. Toast, North Carolina
6. Dividend, Utah
7. Oddville, Kentucky
8. Ink, Arkansas
9. Rough and Ready, California

10. Start, Louisiana
11. Hot Coffee, Mississippi
12. Sleepy Eye, Minnesota
13. Gnaw Bone, Indiana
14. Jackpot, Nevada
15. Truth or Consequences, New Mexico
16. Drain, Oregon
17. Cash, Texas
18. Central Garage, Virginia
19. Ten Sleep, Wyoming
20. Loudville, Massachusetts

8.8

Answers to Instructional Activity 8.1

Diesel, guppy, maverick, melba toast, salmonella, saxophone, and *tetrazzini* are eponyms. *Barracuda, caboose, gavel, kilt,* and *newt* are not.

Answers to Instructional Activity 8.3

Cheddar is named for the village of Cheddar, England; *Colby,* for Colby, Wisconsin; *Edam,* for the town of Edam in the Netherlands; *Emmental,* for the Swiss region of Emmental; *Gorgonzola,* for the Italian village of Gorgonzola; *Gruyère,* for the Swiss town of Gruyère; *Parmesan,* for Parma, Italy; *Roquefort,* for the French village of Roquefort-sur-Soulzon; and *Stilton,* for the English village of Stilton.

Answers to Instructional Activity 8.5

1. D., Denver, The Mile High City
2. E., Detroit, Motor City
3. F., Hollywood, Tinseltown
4. G., International Falls, The Nation's Refrigerator
5. H., Los Angeles, The City of Angels
6. A., New Orleans, The Big Easy
7. C., Pittsburgh, Steel City
8. B., St. Louis, Gateway to the West

Answers to Instructional Activity 8.6

1. E., Wisconsin
2. G., Oklahoma
3. I., North Carolina
4. F., Delaware
5. A., Indiana
6. H., Massachusetts
7. C., New Jersey
8. J., Wyoming
9. D., Ohio
10. B., Kansas

Notes

1. Al Ries and Laura Ries, *The Fall of Advertising and the Rise of PR* (New York: Harper-Collins, 2002), p. 183.

2. Ibid., p. 188.

3. Del I. Hawkins, Roger J. Best, and Kenneth A. Coney, *Consumer Behavior: Building Marketing Strategy*, 9th ed. (New York: McGraw-Hill, 2004), p. 299.

4. Brian Wansink, *Mindless Eating* (New York: Bantam Dell, 2006 [reprinted in 2007]), pp. 125, 126.

5. Deborah Grossman, "Word of Mouth: Menu Descriptors Are the Ultimate Cues for Flavor Expectation, So Choose Them Wisely," Summer 2008, http://www.flavor-online .com.

6. Dale D. Johnson, Bonnie Johnson, Stephen J. Farenga, and Daniel Ness, *Stop High Stakes Testing: An Appeal to America's Conscience* (Lanham, MD: Rowman & Littlefield, 2008), pp. 75–75.

7. Bill Bryson, *Made in America: An Informal History of the English Language in the United States* (New York: William Morrow, 1994), p. 109.

8. Patricia Wen, "E-Mail Address May Be Sending Wrong Message," *Boston Globe* Online, 2000, http://www.boston.com/dailyglobe2/ . . . may_be_sending_wrong_message +.shtml.

9. Paul Dickson, *What's in a Name? Reflections of an Irrepressible Name Collector* (Springfield, MA: Merriam-Webster, 1996).

10. Silla Brush, "They Are What They Teach," *The Chronicle of Higher Education*, June 10, 2005, p. A6.

11. Pat Forbis and Sue Bartolucci, *Stedman's Medical Eponyms*, 2nd ed. (Baltimore, MD: Lippincott Williams & Wilkins, 2005).

12. Auriel Douglas, *Webster's New World Dictionary of Eponyms: Common Words from Proper Nouns* (New York: Simon & Schuster, 1990); Eugene Ehrlich, *What's in a Name? How Proper Names Became Everyday Words* (Darby, PA: Diane Publishing Company, 1999); Morton Freeman, *A New Dictionary of Eponyms* (Oxford, UK: Oxford University Press, 1997); Bonnie Johnson, *Wordworks: Exploring Language Play* (Golden, CO: Fulcrum Publishing, 1999); Laura Lee, *The Name's Familiar* (Gretna, LA: Pelican Publishing Company, 1999).

13. Douglas, *Webster's New World Dictionary of Eponyms*; Freeman, *A New Dictionary of Eponyms*; Johnson, *Wordworks*.

14. Paul Dickson, *Labels for Locals: What to Call People from Abilene to Zimbabwe* (Springfield, MA: Merriam-Webster, 1997), p. x.

15. Ibid., pp. 11, 17, 29, 46, 48, 65, 67, 87, 93, 135, 140, 157, 216, 238.

16. Dickson, *What's in a Name?*

17. Michael D. Shook, *By Any Other Name* (New York: Prentice-Hall, 1994), p. 81.

18. Andrew Delahunty, *Oxford Dictionary of Nicknames* (Oxford, UK: Oxford University Press, 2003); Shook, *By Any Other Name*.

19. Quoted in Dickson, *What's in a Name?*

20. "Scotland: Lost Forever," *New York Times*, February 28, 2004, p. A4.

21. Dan Barry, "In a Town Called Bill, a Boomlet of Sorts," *New York Times*, March 3, 2008, p. A13.

22. Dale D. Johnson, Bonnie Johnson, and Kahleen Schlichting, "Logology: Word and Language Play," in *Vocabulary Instruction: Research to Practice*, ed. James F. Baumann and Edward J. Kame´enui, 179–200 (New York: Guilford Press, 2004).

23. Frank Gallant, *A Place Called Peculiar: Stories About Unusual American Place-Names* (Springfield, MA: Merriam-Webster, 1998).

Word Play

Riddles and Rhymes

Can you solve the following riddles? The answer to each will be a pair of one- or two-syllable rhyming words.

One Syllable
1. What do you call a water mark in a sink?
2. What is an airship for a popular shellfish?
3. What do you call a timepiece made out of stone?
4. What are stingy lambs called?
5. Where would you find hot dogs in a vault?
6. What is the nose of a rainbow fish called?

Two Syllable
7. What could you call the driver of a small lawn pest?
8. What could you call someone who lifts "pearly" mollusks?
9. What is a group of three small waves?
10. What is the strength that is derived from a gentle rain?
11. How could you describe a sticky stomach?
12. What could you call someone who gets fewer of these riddles correct?

These special riddles are a type of word play called *hink pinks* (one-syllable rhyming words) and *hinky pinkies* (two-syllable rhyming words). The answers to the hink pinks and hinky pinkies above are:

1. a drain stain

2. a shrimp blimp
3. a rock clock
4. cheap sheep
5. a frank bank
6. a trout snout
7. a gopher chauffeur
8. an oyster hoister
9. a triple ripple
10. shower power
11. a gummy tummy
12. a lesser guesser

Word play refers to the adaptation or use of words for enjoyment and learning, and it is accomplished by manipulating the meanings, sounds, formations, and positions of words and letters within words. Word play serves several critical purposes in the home and at school. We consider just two of these here. (1) From birth, children exhibit a natural interest in language and an instinct for language.[1] Language is a source of excitement and pleasure to children. They often explore and experiment with the sounds, the nuances, and the unpredictable qualities of language. Accordingly, many young children enjoy word-play games of all types. (2) American English is laced with word-play devices, so it is imperative that learners be able to interpret and produce these linguistic manipulations in oral and written language.

It is worthwhile, therefore, for teachers to incorporate word- and language-play activities in the classroom to stimulate and sustain children's innate interest and expand their base for language comprehension and productivity. Such activities are all too often not the case. As linguist David Crystal has lamented:

> Given the high profile of language play within adult society, its prominence during the years when children are learning to speak, and its relevance to literacy and verbal art, you would naturally expect that it would have a privileged place in those materials and settings where children are being taught to read and write, or to develop their abilities in the use of

spoken language. You would expect reading schemes to soak themselves thoroughly in it. You would expect authors writing for very young children to make copious use of it. You would expect curriculum documents to draw special attention to it. Well, if you do have these expectations, you will be severely disappointed. For when we look for ludic [i.e., playful] language in the books and materials which children have traditionally encountered in school, while learning to develop their abilities in listening, speaking, reading, and writing . . . we . . . find next to nothing there.[2]

Given today's intensive emphasis on high-stakes test preparation in public schools, there is reason to worry that valuable word-play experiences will take an even further backseat in classrooms.

Hink pink riddles probably have been around as long as language itself. No one knows when they first were used. In recent decades, interest in these riddles has strengthened, and they have been described and exemplified by numerous researchers.[3]

Regardless of their labels (e.g., *hank panks, hinky pinkies*), the idea behind these riddles is the same: In response to a question or a definition, the answer must be a pair of rhyming words. Some hink pink riddles are simple (e.g., an overweight rodent is a *fat rat*, a warm kettle is a *hot pot*). Others are relatively difficult (e.g., a melting error is a *thaw flaw*, to bite into cabbage salad is to *gnaw slaw*). A similar range of difficulties exists for hinky pinkies (e.g., decayed cloth is *rotten cotton*, a chicken supporter is a *rooster booster*).

Hink pink–type riddles contribute to young people's development of several language components: vocabulary and reading comprehension, linguistic challenges, rhyme, differences and similarities in synonyms and related words, and homographs (i.e., multiple-meaning words) and homophones (i.e., words with the same sound but different spellings and meanings). As Linda Gibson Geller points out, solving hink pink riddles "represents an exercise in the descriptive use of language" and "the requirement that the answer be in rhyme and meter stretches the student's linguistic creativity and originality."[4] The effectiveness of these rhyming games has also been noted by child psychologist Margie Golick, who has worked with children struggling with learning problems:

Reading theoreticians and researchers have long suspected a link between children's sensitivity to rhyme and the phonological skills essential in becoming a good reader. . . . In all of the games the
problem-solving element is paramount. While learning to rhyme, to
isolate beginning and ending sounds, and to alphabetize, the players
are learning to solve problems. And while solving them, they are
thinking about words, learning the meanings of new ones, learning
new facts, stretching their memories, and strengthening their powers
of concentration.[5]

What cannot be overstated is that for many language learners, from
preschool through adulthood, the hink pink riddle is just plain fun.
Every teacher knows that when an activity is enjoyable, learning is en-
hanced. We ourselves became interested in the learning potential of hink
pink riddles several years ago while writing a book on reading comprehension. Later, we included hink pink activities in a vocabulary instructional series as well as a word-play instructional series. By the time
that we authored a game based solely on hink pink–type riddles,[6] we had
expanded the riddle format from three "families" of rhyming pairs (one-,
two-, and three-syllable) to nine categories by adding three levels of homographs and three levels of homophones as shown below.

Nine Categories of Riddles in Three Families

The Hink Pink Family

1. Hink pinks are one-syllable rhyming words:
   What would you call a well-used tuba?
   a *worn horn*
2. Hinky pinkies are two-syllable rhyming words:
   How do you refer to a big rock that isn't as young as the one
   next to it?
   the *older boulder*

3. Hinkety pinketies are three-syllable rhyming words:
   What could you call a person who is speaking to a college
   instructor?
   a *professor addresser*

The Hink Hink Family (Homographs)

4. Hink hinks are one-syllable homographs (words with the same
   sound and spelling but different meanings):
   What might you call a lamp that doesn't weigh much?
   a *light light*
5. Hinky hinkies are two-syllable homographs (words with the
   same sound and spelling but different meanings):
   What could you call a small green appetizer that has a pit?
   an *olive olive*
6. Hinkety hinketies are three-syllable homographs (words with
   the same sound and spelling but different meanings):
   What could you call a round handbill or flyer?
   a *circular circular*

The Pink Pink Family (Homophones)

7. Pink pinks are one-syllable homophones (words with the same
   sound but different spellings and meanings):
   What could you call a self-centered artery?
   a *vain vein*
8. Pinky pinkies are two-syllable homophones (words with the
   same sound but different spellings and meanings):
   What could you call a person who lifts shaving implements?
   a *razor raiser*
9. Pinkety pinketies are three-syllable homophones (words with
   the same sound but different spellings and meanings):
   What do you call a story in installments about breakfast grain?
   a *cereal serial*

Instructional Activity   9.1

In the pages that follow, we present numerous riddles with one- and two-syllable rhyming responses. Three-syllable rhyming responses are scarce, but a few are provided for each family. Sometimes the riddle and the answer are plausible (e.g., a *drain stain* and a *lesser guesser*). More often, the riddles and their answers will be silly—but still instructive—and that is what makes solving them such a popular form of word play and learning. Individuals or teams can engage in contests to see who can solve the most riddles or how quickly they can solve them. Difficulty usually—but not always—increases with the number of syllables, and the pink pink family riddles tend to be more challenging than the hink pink or hink hink family riddles.

Teachers or parents who are interested in creating their own hink pink–type riddles will find that a rhyming dictionary is useful. Our favorite is *Words to Rhyme With: A Rhyming Dictionary.*[7] This work includes more than 80,000 words that rhyme, such as *eke, beak, Mozambique, cheek, chic, sheik, batik,* and *triptyque.*

The answers to all of the following riddles are at the end of the chapter.

9.1

Hink Pinks

The answers to hink pink riddles are two one-syllable rhyming words.

Example: What could you call a tardy platter?
Answer: a *late plate*

What could you call:

1. celery conversation?
2. an uninteresting health resort?
3. embarrassment about your label?
4. a talking parrot?

   5. a strict wetland?
   6. an exam for a rat or cockroach?
   7. a pickup full of quackers?
   8. a certain bashful insect?
   9. things that aren't smooth?
  10. the group that meets at noon?
  11. squashed Cheddar and mozzarella?
  12. a little dance done by a small branch?
  13. a money conflict?
  14. a seat for a rabbit?
  15. a cozy carpet?
  16. a grumpy person's sofa?
  17. an animal doctor who works mostly with fish?
  18. a fancy dress worn only in the city?
  19. a little poem about a green citrus fruit?
  20. an agitated creek?
  21. the sudden pulling of a wooden board?
  22. business attire for an owl?
  23. the surprise of a watch?
  24. one piece of wet postage?
  25. a first-rate group of hogs?
  26. a cunning dessert with a crust?
  27. the origin of the route?
  28. a single rock?
  29. an unusual fabric rip?
  30. the trading of stores?
  31. a large excavation?
  32. a bag for treats?
  33. the avoidance of a certain type of joke?
  34. a journey by boat?
  35. a stuck-up ear of corn?
  36. the messiest person in a group of unruly people?
  37. a squashed cap?
  38. a boat that an insect would use to pull a big ship?

39. someone who steals T-bones and sirloins?
40. a skinny smile?
41. a group of undecorated cars?
42. a stinker's suitcase?
43. a shy stream?
44. a streetcar for a certain type of shellfish?
45. a ten-cent poem?
46. an unhappy boy?
47. a certain bird of prey's stroll?
48. a book designed to help women who are getting married?
49. the meals served at a ranch for city folks?
50. a mild controlled fire?
51. an update on certain footwear?
52. an unusual swoon?
53. soreness caused by too much wiggling?
54. a jet runway?
55. a tree with acorns that has no money?
56. a quick explosion?
57. a sad buddy?
58. the leader of a gang of robbers?
59. the nap taken onboard a vacation ship?
60. unusual pocket money?

Hink Hinks

The answers to hink hink riddles are two one-syllable homographs (i.e., multiple-meaning words) with the same spellings and sounds.

Example: What could you call the teasing of a young goat?
Answer: a *kid kid*

What would you call:

1. the fenced-in area for ballpoints?
2. a popular shellfish that is very tiny?

3. legal action about a type of business attire?
4. a certain flower that keeps quiet?
5. a sheet of canvas that goes on a voyage?
6. the fast departure of a roll of cloth?
7. the thwarting of a fencing sword?
8. the most important map legend?
9. a tasty crustacean that is a grump?
10. a shrub and flower factory?
11. a high-quality group of students?
12. the food eaten by a white worm?
13. a nervous verb form?
14. gravel courage?
15. a prairie stove?
16. fights over dinner leftovers?
17. the carefree adventure of a songbird?
18. the piece of furniture that the committee leader uses?
19. the submerging of an object with faucets?
20. a hyphen race?
21. quick letters about musical tones?
22. the cards dealt to a member of a ship's crew?
23. an error in a geological rift?
24. a fishing tool used by a piece of asparagus?
25. a group of thieves who steal finger jewelry?
26. the act of declining a school promotion?
27. a short news item about a haircut?
28. it when scraggly bushes wash a floor?
29. the distance between two points in galaxies?
30. a tropical tree that fits in the hand?
31. an underweight lamp?
32. the crushing of a harvest vegetable?
33. it when strawberry and marmalade play music all night?
34. a solid, immovable business?
35. an elephant snout's suitcase?
36. the evasion of a question by a thick row of bushes?

37. the thin coating on a motion picture?
38. a piece of legislation about a restaurant check?
39. a wise person's favorite seasoning?
40. a cast-aside storage building?

Pink Pinks

The answers to pink pink riddles are two one-syllable homophones—words that have the same sound but different spellings and meanings.

Example: What could you call a short look at a mountaintop?
Answer: a *peak peek*

What could you call:

1. a pleasant group of connected hotel rooms?
2. a just-born African antelope?
3. a forbidden musical group?
4. an animal with a gravelly voice?
5. the actual fishing spool?
6. the duty on short nails?
7. a reasonable taxi fee?
8. a weather instrument's blood vessel?
9. a nearly colorless bucket?
10. a banned poet?
11. a survey taken by a slender post?
12. a squeezed piece of a ladder?
13. a corn puzzle?
14. a track-and-field competition for lamb, pork, and beef?
15. a tired reddish-purple vegetable?
16. an inexpensive chirp?
17. the period when precipitation rules?
18. a precious doe?
19. the light drizzle for which you were lonesome?
20. the ocean trip taken by ship workers?

21. a musical selection about the absence of war?
22. a spoiled chicken?
23. an evening for a medieval soldier?
24. an uninterested piece of lumber?
25. an arrogant device for wind?
26. the cry of a large ocean mammal?
27. two of the same fruit?
28. the money it takes to buy an old stringed instrument?
29. money intelligence?
30. the name for a powerful cleaning solution's fib?
31. a common chimney illness?
32. a narrow passage of water that is not crooked?
33. someone's share in a T-bone business?
34. the king's chair when it was tossed?
35. a boyfriend's necktie?

Hinky Pinkies

The answers to hinky pinky riddles are two two-syllable rhyming words.

Example: What could you call a jolly currant?
Answer: a *merry berry*

What could you call:

1. a leisurely excursion through the prickly shrubbery?
2. a convicted cantaloupe criminal?
3. someone who plays the guitar only between spring and fall?
4. a cow that tells on other cows?
5. a violin puzzle?
6. astonishing foot racing?
7. dusk seen through a roof window?
8. an enjoyment gauge?
9. one piece of roof covering?
10. a soap opera about a South American pack animal?

11. the looting of a tiny town?
12. an argument in the palace?
13. a cart pulled by an imaginary beast?
14. the evil laughter of a wild, doglike animal?
15. an odd-behaving gobbler?
16. the person who purchased something before you did?
17. the movement of numerators and denominators?
18. the special language of a popular game of chance?
19. learning gained from a university?
20. the work done by the people next door?
21. the more modest acrobat?
22. a problem with thin paper?
23. a frightening grassland?
24. a person who is a faster harvester?
25. a person who is searching for a tennis shoe?
26. a certain thin bird?
27. someone who ruins a certain round gameboard piece?
28. a boat that takes milk products back and forth across a bay?
29. a tinier carrier?
30. an out-of-shape kitten?
31. a lobster that won't share?
32. the movement of the sea?
33. the container for a large rock?
34. the person who piles crisp wafers?
35. a tale about honor and renown?
36. a sports coat for a tennis paddle?
37. a person who instructs from a grandstand?
38. a more hip king?
39. the theft of stationery?
40. an afflicted hen?
41. someone who demonstrates against a chirping insect?
42. a damper cardigan?
43. a person who pounds a mallet too hard?

44. a particular legume that is kind and tender?
45. a person who goes to a store to buy a frog?

Hinky Hinkies

The answers to hinky hinky riddles are two homographs—words that have the same spelling and sound but different meanings.

Example: What could you call a TV station's waterway?
Answer: a *channel channel.*

What could you call:

1. it when boards of wood walk awkwardly?
2. a ship's device that reads the news?
3. the 1/60th of a minute that comes after the first one?
4. an artist's ideal subject?
5. the noise made by a tennis paddle?
6. a nation that is totally rural?
7. the tax classification of a shelf support?
8. the purpose of a social gathering?
9. a parking violation given to a slate of election candidates?
10. a gulp by a certain common bird?
11. a gift that is here right now?
12. a intestinal punctuation mark?
13. a big, burly sled dog?
14. interfering with a large basket of laundry?
15. the center of the eye of a student?
16. the junk produced by a group of puppies?
17. a regular article about a supporting pillar?
18. a demand for tidiness?
19. an unusual fiction book?
20. the struggle of a certain fish?
21. an experimental courtroom process?

22. the organization in charge of a chest of drawers?
23. a group of experts who discuss a rectangular board?
24. the insect mascot of a British game similar to baseball?
25. a measuring device that records units of length?

Pinky Pinkies

The answers to pinky pinky riddles are two two-syllable homophones—words that have the same sound but different spellings and meanings.

Example: What could you call a basement salesperson?
Answer: a *cellar seller*

What could you call:

1. a person who talks rhythmically to music about the paper around a candy bar?
2. a slender candle used by a three-toed, long-snouted animal?
3. a donkey tunnel?
4. the hearsay told about a boardinghouse resident?
5. a singing reef?
6. a very strange public market?
7. the selling of a bicycle part?
8. the strength of a certain kind of shellfish?
9. a person who stays in a rooming house on an international boundary?
10. a berry that is up-to-date?

Three-syllable responses to these riddles are harder to come by. Here are just a few to challenge your best problem-solving skills and vocabulary knowledge.

Hinkety Pinketies

Hinkety pinketies are three-syllable rhyming words.

What could you call:

1. a "how-to" book that comes out every year?
2. the White House?
3. a determination reached with exactness?
4. the answer to contamination?
5. just average boredom?
6. a large, colorful handkerchief worn by a yellow fruit?

Hinkety Hinketies

Hinkety hinketies are three-syllable homographs.
What could you call:

1. an orbital movement around a citizen uprising?
2. an extreme sadness caused by a severe recession?
3. the agency in charge of sales bonuses?
4. the foremost school-building administrator in the district?
5. an everlasting hairsetting?

Pinkety Pinketies

Pinkety pinketies are three-syllable homophones.
What could you call:

1. motionless writing paper?
2. the main rule?
3. a funny arm bone?

All of the preceding riddles were answered with a modifier-noun combination. The riddles also can be constructed so that the response requires a verb-object combination. Here are just a few examples.

Hink Pinks

Example: What does someone do who turns over boats?
Answer: That person *flips ships*.

1. What does a person do who manufactures stopping devices?
2. What do you do when you pester Colby, Parmesan, and Edam?
3. What do you do when you talk back to a lawn?

Hinky Pinkies

Example: What does someone do who looks at canned fruit?
Answer: That person *observes preserves.*

1. What could you call the act of helping with a pigtail?
2. What does someone do who watches appetizers?
3. What does someone do who risks being quickly seen?
4. What do you do when you clap your hands overseas?

Hink Hinks

Example: What does someone do who hits stockings?
Answer: That person *socks socks.*

1. What does a teacher do who checks punctuation marks?
2. What does someone do who plows cash register drawers?

Hinky Hinkies

Example: What is someone doing who is stacking pier poles?
Answer: That person is *piling piling.*

1. What do you do when you really enjoy chopped pickles on a hot dog?

Pink Pinks

Example: What do you do when you elevate sun beams?
Answer: You *raise rays.*

1. What does a doctor do who cures cads?
2. What does someone do who transports corridors?
3. What does someone do who looks at oceans?

4. When you compose sentences without mistakes, what do you do?

Whatever a student's level of literacy development, it can be heightened by improving his or her fascination with language. Two sure ways to develop a love of language are to read good books often and to engage in word-play activities. Hink pink riddles help to expand students' cultural literacy backgrounds, enabling them to learn from their teachers, from one another, and from books, media, and the world around them. The riddles are challenging and thought provoking. They offer varied opportunities for examining and responding to the nuances of vocabulary, and they provide the enjoyment that comes from rhyme.

Answers to Hink Pink Riddles

1. stalk talk
2. a blah spa
3. name shame
4. a word bird
5. a harsh marsh
6. a pest test
7. a duck truck
8. a shy fly
9. rough stuff
10. the lunch bunch
11. a cheese squeeze
12. a twig jig
13. a cash clash
14. a hare chair
15. a snug rug
16. a grouch couch
17. a wet vet
18. a town gown
19. a lime rhyme
20. a shook brook
21. a plank yank

22. a hoot suit
23. clock shock
24. a damp stamp
25. fine swine
26. a sly pie
27. the course source
28. a lone stone
29. a rare tear
30. a shop swap
31. a big dig
32. a snack sack
33. a pun shun
34. a ship trip
35. a cob snob
36. the mob slob
37. a flat hat
38. a bug tug
39. a beef thief
40. a thin grin
41. a plain train
42. a skunk trunk
43. a meek creek
44. a clam tram
45. a dime rhyme
46. a sad lad
47. a hawk walk
48. a bride guide
49. dude food
50. a tame flame
51. shoes news
52. a quaint faint
53. a shake ache
54. a plane lane
55. a broke oak

56. a fast blast
57. a glum chum
58. the chief thief
59. a cruise snooze
60. strange change

Answers to Hink Hink Riddles

1. a pen pen
2. a shrimp shrimp
3. a suit suit
4. a mum mum
5. a sail sail
6. a bolt bolt
7. a foil foil
8. the key key
9. a crab crab
10. a plant plant
11. a class class
12. grub grub
13. a tense tense
14. grit grit
15. a range range
16. scraps scraps
17. a lark lark
18. the chair chair
19. a sink sink
20. a dash dash
21. notes notes
22. a hand hand
23. a fault fault
24. a spear spear
25. a ring ring
26. a pass pass
27. a clip clip

28. a scrub scrub
29. space space
30. a palm palm
31. a light light
32. a squash squash
33. a jam jam
34. a firm firm
35. a trunk trunk
36. a hedge hedge
37. film film
38. a bill bill
39. sage sage
40. a shed shed

Answers to Pink Pink Riddles

1. a sweet suite
2. a new gnu
3. a banned band
4. a hoarse horse
5. the real reel
6. a tacks tax
7. a fair fare
8. a vain vein
9. a pale pail
10. a barred bard
11. a pole poll
12. a wrung rung
13. a maize maze
14. a meat meet
15. a beat beet
16. a cheap cheep
17. the rain reign
18. a dear deer
19. the missed mist

20. the crew's cruise
21. a peace piece
22. a foul fowl
23. a knight night
24. a bored board
25. a vain vane
26. a whale wail
27. a pear pair
28. lute loot
29. cents sense
30. a lye lie
31. the flue flu
32. a straight strait
33. a steak stake
34. the thrown throne
35. a beau bow

Answers to Hinky Pinky Riddles

1. a bramble ramble
2. a melon felon
3. a summer strummer
4. a cattle tattle
5. a fiddle riddle
6. stunning running
7. skylight twilight
8. a pleasure measure
9. a single shingle
10. a llama drama
11. a village pillage
12. a castle hassle
13. a dragon wagon
14. a jackal cackle
15. a quirky turkey
16. the prior buyer

17. fraction action
18. bingo lingo
19. college knowledge
20. neighbor labor
21. a humbler tumbler
22. a tissue issue
23. a scary prairie
24. a quicker picker
25. a sneaker seeker
26. a narrow sparrow
27. a checker wrecker
28. a dairy ferry
29. a smaller hauler
30. a flabby tabby
31. a selfish shellfish
32. ocean motion
33. the boulder holder
34. a cracker stacker
35. a glory story
36. a racket jacket
37. a bleacher teacher
38. a cooler ruler
39. a paper caper
40. a stricken chicken
41. a cricket picket
42. a wetter sweater
43. a hammer slammer
44. a gentle lentil
45. a hopper shopper

Answers to Hinky Hinky Riddles

1. lumber lumber
2. an anchor anchor

3. the second second
4. a model model
5. a racket racket
6. a country country
7. a bracket bracket
8. the function function
9. a ticket ticket
10. a swallow swallow
11. a present present
12. a colon colon
13. a husky husky
14. a hamper hamper
15. the pupil pupil
16. litter litter
17. a column column
18. an order order
19. a novel novel
20. a flounder flounder
21. a trial trial
22. the bureau bureau
23. a panel panel
24. the cricket cricket
25. a meter meter

Answers to Pinky Pinky Riddles

1. a wrapper rapper
2. a tapir taper
3. a burro burrow
4. a roomer rumor
5. a choral coral
6. a bizarre bazaar
7. a pedal peddle
8. mussel muscle

9. a border boarder
10. the current currant

Answers to Hinkety Pinkety Riddles

1. the annual manual
2. the president's residence
3. a precision decision
4. the pollution solution
5. medium tedium
6. a banana bandana

Answers to Hinkety Hinkety Riddles

1. a revolution revolution
2. a depression depression
3. the commission commission
4. the principal principal
5. a permanent permanent

Answers to Pinkety Pinkety Riddles

1. stationary stationery
2. the principal principle
3. a humorous humerus

Answers to Verb-Object Riddles

Hink Pinks

1. That person makes brakes.
2. You tease cheese.
3. You sass grass.

Hinky Pinkies

1. That person is aiding braiding.
2. That person observes hors d'oeuvres.
3. That person chances glances.
4. You applaud abroad.

Hink Hinks

1. The teacher marks marks.
2. That person tills tills.

Hinky Hinkies

1. You relish relish.

Pink Pinks

1. The doctor heals heels.
2. That person hauls halls.
3. That person sees seas.
4. You write right.

Notes

1. Steven Pinker, *The Language Instinct: How the Mind Creates Language* (New York: William Morrow, 1994).

2. David Crystal, *Language Play* (Chicago: University of Chicago Press, 1998), p. 182.

3. See, for example, P. David Pearson and Dale D. Johnson, *Teaching Reading Comprehension* (New York: Holt, Rinehart and Winston, 1987); Gyles Brandreth, *The Joy of Lex* (New York: William Morrow, 1980); Marilyn Burns and Martha Weston, *The Hink Pink Book* (Boston: Little, Brown, 1981); Tony Augarde, *The Oxford Guide to Word Games* (Oxford, UK: Oxford University Press, 1984); Linda Gibson Geller, *Wordplay and Language Learning for Children* (Urbana, IL: National Council of Teachers of English, 1985); Dale D. Johnson and Bonnie Johnson, *Ginn Vocabulary Series* (Lexington, MA: Ginn and Company, 1986); Dale D. Johnson and Bonnie Johnson, *In So Many Words* Series (Logan, IA: Perfection Learning, 1990); Dale D. Johnson and Bonnie Johnson, *The Brain Train* Game (Elizabethtown, PA: Continental Press, 1994); Margie Golick, *Playing with Words* (Markham, ON: Pembroke Publishers, 1987); Richard Lederer, *Get Thee to a Punnery* (Charleston, SC: Wyrick, 1988); Bonnie Johnson, *Wordworks: Exploring Language Play* (Golden, CO: Fulcrum Publishing, 1999); and Dave Morice, *The Dictionary of Word Play* (New York: Teachers & Writers Collaborative, 2001).

4. Geller, *Wordplay and Language Learning for Children*, p. 77.

5. Golick, *Playing with Words*, pp. 26–27.

6. Johnson and Johnson, *The Brain Train* Game.

7. Willard R. Espy and Orrin Hargraves, *Words to Rhyme With: A Rhyming Dictionary*, 3rd ed. (New York: Checkmark Books, 2006).

A Mélange of Words in Language and Life

The difference between the right word and the almost right word is really a large matter. It's the difference between lightning and the lightning bug.

—Mark Twain (1888)

A speaker or writer's choice of words is the heart of the message. Words signify the ideas, feelings, and purposes of the user. The difference between talented speakers and writers and those less so is their ability to choose just the right word to convey with precision the meaning that they intend.

We close this volume with a look at words used well. This capstone to our journey through word origins and formations, figurative language and proverbs, semantic connections, names, games, and ambiguity is a potpourri of catchphrases, slogans, and sayings memorable for their lasting impact, their wisdom, or their wit. We have included some words that were spoken too soon. Also included are examples that show what words can do when chosen with care by speakers and writers who understand the power of words.

Catchphrases

A *catchphrase* is a phrase used so frequently by particular individuals, groups, or cultural entities that it locks onto people's attention and becomes part of our linguistic landscape. Some catchphrases (e.g., *I've arrived and to prove it I'm here*) are ephemeral and disappear from use after a time. Others (e.g., *Last of the big spenders*) tend to endure. Catchphrases emanate from literature, politics, sports, films, and popular culture. No one knows why certain catchphrases catch on. Some of them rhyme or use alliteration, but others do not. Repetition is a requirement, whether it is the intentional repetition used by political advisers or the oft-repeated lines of a television character. The term *catchphrase* can be traced to the mid-nineteenth century.[1] Catchphrases originally were regarded as phrases that appeal to the unsophisticated or immature reader or listener, and that assessment may be true today to some degree.

Some U.S. presidents and their staffs have strived to create lofty catchphrases that brand their administrations by encompassing their major goals. Several of the catchphrases caught on and still are used when that president is discussed. Others just never "grabbed" the population. Have you heard any of the following presidential catchphrases?

Woodrow Wilson	*A New Freedom*
Theodore Roosevelt	*A Square Deal*
Franklin Delano Roosevelt	*A New Deal*
Harry Truman	*A Fair Deal*
John F. Kennedy	*The New Frontier*
Lyndon Johnson	*The Great Society*
William Clinton	*A New Covenant*
George W. Bush	*An Ownership Society*
Barak Obama	*A New Foundation*

According to Peter Baker, "More recent presidents have had trouble making their labels stick. Clinton's *New Covenant* was dropped on the advice of pollsters, and Bush's *Ownership Society* . . . made little impression."[2] The jury is out on Obama's *New Foundation*.

Here are some other catchphrases from popular culture:[3]

Ain't nobody here but us chickens (1947)
(It's) all done with mirrors (1900)

And awa-a-aay we go! (1952)
Another day, another dollar (1910)
As if! (1995)
Back to square one! (1930s)
Beam me up, Scottie (1966)
Bells and whistles (1984)
Big Brother is watching (1949)
(The) bigger they come, the harder they fall (1900)
(The) buck stops here (1945)
Cheap at half the price (1800s)
Cry all the way to the bank (1973)
(The) customer is always right (1909)
Don't call us, we'll call you (1961)
Don't get mad, get even (1961)
Don't worry, be happy (1988)
Eat your heart out! (1950s)
Garbage in, garbage out (1960s)
Go ahead, make my day (1983)
(The) greatest thing since sliced bread (1920s)
(A) hard act to follow (1900s)
Here's another fine mess you've gotten me into (1930)
How sweet it is (1952)
If you can't stand the heat, get out of the kitchen (1960s)
I'll take a rain check (1940s)
Just what the doctor ordered (1910s)
Let's get down to the nitty gritty (1963)
(There is) no such thing as a free lunch (1840s)
—, not! (1989)
On a scale of one to ten (1977)
One step forward, two steps back (1904)
Show me the money! (1996)
(The) sixty-four thousand dollar question (1950s)
Take the money and run (1968)
When the going gets tough, the tough get going (1962)

Works for me (1984)
You can run, but you can't hide (1946)

Slogans

Slogans are short, catchy phrases created to promote a purpose, product, person, or point of view. Ideally, they are also memorable. The sheer marketing objective of slogans is what differentiates them from catchphrases; they do not become popular accidentally as is the case with most catchphrases. Slogans are used primarily in advertising and political campaigning, and they are designed to stick in your mind. In the introduction to her compendium of slogans, Janet Braunstein wrote, "Slogans are all around us, on TV and radio commercials, on billboards, in magazines and newspapers, on the bottles, cans, boxes and bags that fill our cupboards and closets."[4] Add to those the slogans found on the Internet and in the e-mails, voicemails, text messages, and tweets that we receive. As with everything, some slogans are more effective than others. The following slogans were intended to sway voters in presidential elections. Their ostensible purpose was to describe a policy or a set of programs proposed or implemented. Some were authorized by the candidate, but others originated with supporters or the media.

Date	Candidate	Slogan
1864	Abraham Lincoln	*Don't swap horses in the middle of a stream*
1892	Benjamin Harrison	*Grover, Grover, All Is Over*
1900	William McKinley	*A Full Dinner Pail*
1916	Woodrow Wilson	*He kept us out of war*
1920	Warren G. Harding	*Return to Normalcy*
1928	Herbert Hoover	*A Chicken in Every Pot, A Car in Every Garage*
1932	Franklin D. Roosevelt	*In Hoover We Trusted, Now We Are Busted*
1940	Wendell Willkie	*Roosevelt for Ex-President*
1944	John Dewey	*Dewey or Don't We?*

1948	Harry Truman	*Phooey on Dewey*
1952	Dwight D. Eisenhower	*I Like Ike*
	Adlai Stevenson	*We're Madly for Adlai*
1956	Adlai Stevenson	*Vote Gladly for Adlai*
	Dwight D. Eisenhower	*The Might Tower—Eisenhower*
1960	John F. Kennedy	*Nix on Nixon*
1964	Lyndon B. Johnson	*USA for LBJ*
		Help Barry Stamp Out Peace
1968	Hubert Humphrey	*Nixon + Spiro = Zero*
	Richard Nixon	*Dump the Hump*
1976	Jimmy Carter	*Not Just Peanuts*
1988	George H. W. Bush	*Read My Lips, No New Taxes*
1992	Ross Perot	*Ross for Boss*
2008	Barack Obama	*Change We Can Believe In*

Instructional Activity 10.1

Below are several slogans from American history. Select three of the slogans and conduct research on the stories behind them. These stories can be shared during a class session.

No taxation without representation. (1763)
Give me liberty or give me death. (1775)
We must all hang together, or most assuredly we shall all hang separately. (1776)
Tippecanoe and Tyler too (1840)
A house divided against itself cannot stand. (1858)
With malice toward none, with charity for all (1865)
Give me your tired, your poor. (1883)
Speak softly and carry a big stick. (1901)
Prosperity is just around the corner. (1930)
I shall return. (1942)
Ich bin ein Berliner. (1963)

10.1

Words Spoken Too Soon

Some experts have been willing to share their insights, express opinions, or make predictions. Well-chosen words can make an impression, sometimes lasting, but they are not always accurate. The following quotations were documented by the Institute of Expertology and published in its collection *The Experts Speak: The Definitive Compendium of Authoritative Misinformation.*[5] Despite the expertise or stature of the speaker or writer, the choice of just the right words, and the eloquence of the delivery, some of these observations did not hold water.

"Bees are generated from decomposed veal." (The scholar St. Isidore of Seville in the seventh century A.D.)

"We do not believe in the permanence of his reputation. . . . Fifty years hence . . . our children will wonder what their ancestors could have meant by putting Mr. (Charles) Dickens at the head of the novelists of his day." (London's *The Saturday Review*, 1858)

"X-rays are a hoax." (British scientist Lord Kelvin)

"The horse is here to stay, but the automobile is only a novelty—a fad." (Michigan banker Horace Rackham, 1903)

"Airplanes will be used in sport, but they are not to be thought of as commercial carriers." (Engineer Octave Chanute, 1904)

"Experimental evidence is strongly in favor of my argument that the chemical purity of the air is of no importance." (Physiology lecturer L. Erskine Hill, London Hospital, 1912)

"While theoretically and technically television may be feasible, commercially and financially I consider it an impossibility, a development of which we need waste little time dreaming." (American inventor Lee DeForest, 1926)

"There is as much chance of repealing the 18th Amendment [prohibition] as there is for a humming-bird to fly to the planet Mars with the Washington Monument tied to its tail." (Senator Morris Sheppard, 1930)

"I think there is a world market for about five computers." (Thomas Watson, chairman of IBM, 1943)

"You ain't goin' nowhere . . . son. You ought to go back to drivin' a truck." (Manager of the Grand Ole Opry who fired Elvis Presley in 1954)

Words That Have Lasted

Other sayings have lasted and are cited often because of their insight, wisdom, or common sense. Here are some examples.

"Experience is a hard teacher. She gives the test first." (Anonymous)

"People will believe anything if you whisper it." (Anonymous)

"If you are not part of the solution, you are part of the problem." (Eldridge Cleaver)

"Nothing in life is to be feared. It is only to be understood." (Marie Curie)

"Common sense is genius dressed in its working clothes." (Ralph Waldo Emerson)

"Truth is such a rare thing, it is delightful to tell it." (Emily Dickinson)

"The only thing more expensive than education is ignorance." (Benjamin Franklin)

"No one can make you feel inferior without your consent." (Eleanor Roosevelt)

"The only certainty is that nothing is certain." (Pliny the Elder)

"Everyone is ignorant only on different subjects." (Will Rogers)

"It has ever been my experience that folks who have no vices have very few virtues." (Abraham Lincoln)

Retronyms

In concluding this volume, we return to the thesis of our first chapter: American English is an ever-changing language. A trip to a supermarket or some other store shows how language has expanded to accommodate our increasing product specialization. Years ago, a person would go to the grocery store to pick up a quart of milk. Now the variety of milks offered require some decision making. Should you get whole milk or 2 percent or skim milk?

The linguistic term for these modified nouns is *retronym*, defined as "a phrase coined because an expression once used alone needs contrastive qualification: . . . *analog watch* because of *digital watch*. . . . Retronyms emerge when contrast becomes necessary."[6] So, a retronym is a noun that is joined by an adjective to help clarify the original noun and distinguish it from newer, more specialized elaborations of a product or process. Sol Steinmetz and Barbara Ann Kipfer coined the word *neonym* ("new" + "name") to describe new words that, in each case, necessitated converting a word to a retronym (e.g., original word: *soap*, retronym: *bar soap*, neonym: *liquid soap*; original word: *computer*, retronym: *desktop computer*, neonym: *laptop computer*).[7]

Instructional Activity 10.2

Complete the lists below. You might want to visit a grocery or "big box" store to help you with this activity.

Original Word	Retronym	Neonym
television	network television	cable television
skis	snow skis	water skis
diet (noun)		
cracker		
book		
olives		
mustard		
bread		
vinegar		

toothbrush
coffee
water

Our hope is that this book will promote a comparative discussion of research findings that, in turn, will highlight our ever-changing language in an ever-changing society. Words convey the meanings of the world and all its intricacies. Words provide us with expressive strength and the means to understand the thoughts of others. Words are the foundation of literacy.

Notes

1. Anna Farkas, *The Oxford Dictionary of Catchphrases* (Oxford, UK: Oxford University Press, 2002).

2. Peter Baker, "New Deal. Great Society. New Foundation?" *New York Times*, May 16, 2009, p. A8.

3. Nigel Rees, *Dictionary of Catchphrases* (London, UK: Cassell Publishers, 1995); Farkas, *The Oxford Dictionary of Catchphrases.*

4. Laurence Urdang and Janet Braunstein, *Every Bite a Delight and Other Slogans* (Detroit, MI: Visible Ink, 1992), p. x.

5. Christopher Cerf and Victor Navasky, *The Experts Speak: The Definitive Compendium of Authoritative Misinformation* (New York: Pantheon Books, 1984), pp. 38, 68, 152, 183, 206, 208, 228, 238, 303.

6. Tom McArthur, *The Concise Oxford Companion to the English Language* (Oxford, UK: Oxford University Press, 1996), p. 78.

7. Sol Steinmetz and Barbara Ann Kipfer, *The Life of Language* (New York: Random House, 2006), pp. 295–296.

Acknowledgments

There are no incentives for anyone who writes a foreword or preface to a book; therefore, we are especially grateful to renowned scholars Michael Kamil and Jack Cassidy. Their many contributions to the field of literacy are legendary. We have great respect for the talented and professional editorial and design team at Westview Press: Evan Carver and Alex Masulis, Acquisitions Editors; Melissa Veronesi, Production Editor; Christine Arden, Copy Editor; and Brent Wilcox, Designer. Monica and Jim von Hoff of Insight Creative Services took our verbal descriptions and turned them into engaging instructional visuals. The unwavering support and warm hearts of Drs. Steve Farenga, Dan Ness, Mark, and Rex belie the notion of cold New Yorkers.

Bibliography

Airwise.com. 2008. Chicago O'Hare. http://www.airwise.com/airports/us/ORD/ORD _07.html.

Aitchison, Jean. *Words in the Mind: An Introduction to the Mental Lexicon*, 2nd ed. Oxford, UK: Blackwell, 1994.

———. *The Language Web: The Power and Problem of Words*. Cambridge, UK: Cambridge University Press, 1997.

Altmann, Gerry T. M. *The Ascent of Babel: An Exploration of Language, Mind, and Understanding*. Oxford, UK: Oxford University Press, 1997.

American Dialect Society. 1999 Words of the Year, Word of the 1990s. Word of the 20th Century, Word of the Millennium, 2000. http://www.americandialect.org/ index.ph/amerdial/1999_word_of_the_year . . .

———. "*Plutoed*" Voted 2006 Word of the Year by American Dialect Society, 2007. http://www.americandialect.org/Word-of-the-year_2006.pdf.

———. American Dialect Society 2007 Words of the Year Nominations, 2008. http://www.americandialect.org/2007.WOTY.nominations.pdf.

———. American Dialect Society 2008 Word of the Year Is "Bailout," 2009. http:// www.americandialect.org/index.php/amerdial/american_dialect_society_2008 _word_of_the_year_is_bailout/.

Ammer, Christine. *Fighting Words: From War, Rebellion, and Other Combative Capers*. Lincolnwood, IL: NTC Publishing Group, 1989 (reprinted in 1999).

———. *Have a Nice Day—No Problem! A Dictionary of Clichés*. New York: Plume, 1992.

———. *The American Heritage Dictionary of Idioms*. Boston: Houghton Mifflin, 1997.

———. *Cool Cats, Top Dogs, and Other Beastly Expressions*. Boston: Houghton Mifflin, 1999.

Anderson, Richard C., and William E. Nagy. "The Vocabulary Conundrum." *American Educator* (Winter 1992): 14–18, 44–47.

Anton, Jim. *Wise Wacky Proverbs: The Truth Behind Everyday Sayings*. New York: Sterling, 1996.

Augarde, Tony. *The Oxford Guide to Word Games.* Oxford, UK: Oxford University Press, 1984.

August, Diane, and Timothy Shanahan, eds. *Developing Literacy in Second-Language Learners: Report of the National Literacy Panel on Language-Minority Children and Youth.* Mahwah, NJ: Lawrence Erlbaum, 2006.

Ayto, John. *Dictionary of Word Origins.* New York: Arcade Publishing, 1990.

———. *A Century of New Words.* Oxford, UK: Oxford University Press, 1999 (reprinted in 2006 and 2007).

Baker, Peter. "New Deal. Great Society. New Foundation?" *New York Times,* May 16, 2009.

Barnette, Martha. *Ladyfingers & Nun's Tummies: A Lighthearted Look at How Foods Got Their Names.* New York: Times Books, 1997.

Barnhart, David K., and Allan A. Metcalf. *America in So Many Words: Words That Have Shaped America.* Boston: Houghton Mifflin, 1997.

Barnhart, Robert K., ed. *The Barnhart Concise Dictionary of Etymology.* New York: HarperCollins, 1995.

Barry, Dan. "In a Town Called Bill, a Boomlet of Sorts." *New York Times,* March 3, 2008.

Berman, Louis A. *Proverb Wit and Wisdom.* New York: Perigee, 1997.

Brandreth, Gyles. *The Joy of Lex.* New York: William Morrow, 1980.

Brown, Lesley, ed. *The New Shorter Oxford English Dictionary,* 2 vols. Oxford, UK: Oxford University Press, 1973 (reprinted in 1993).

Brush, Silla. "They Are What They Teach." *The Chronicle of Higher Education,* June 10, 2005.

Bryson, Bill. *Made in America: An Informal History of the English Language in the United States.* New York: William Morrow, 1994.

Burns, Marilyn, and Martha Weston. *The Hink Pink Book.* Boston: Little, Brown, 1981.

———. *The Oxford A to Z of Word Games.* Oxford, UK: Oxford University Press, 1994.

Carter, Ronald. *Vocabulary: Applied Linguistic Perspectives.* New York: Routledge, 1987.

Carver, Craig M. *A History of English in Its Own Words.* New York: HarperCollins, 1991.

Cerf, Christopher, and Victor Navasky. *The Experts Speak: The Definitive Compendium of Authoritative Misinformation.* New York: Pantheon Books, 1984.

Chalmers, Irena. *The Great Food Almanac.* San Francisco: Collins, 1994.

Christian, Kay, Jane Roberts, Michael Samuels, and Irene Wetherspoon, eds. *Historical Thesaurus of the Oxford English Dictionary.* Oxford, UK: Oxford University Press, 2009.

Clark, Eve V. *Cambridge Studies in Linguistics: The Lexicon in Acquisition.* Cambridge, UK: Cambridge University Press, 1993.

Collier, V. P. "Age and Rate of Acquisition of Language for Academic Purposes." *TESOL Quarterly* 21, no. 4 (1987): 677–741.

Cornu, Anne-Marie. "The First Step in Vocabulary Teaching." *Modern Language Journal* 63 (1979): 262–272.

Crystal, David. *The Cambridge Encyclopedia of the English Language.* Cambridge, UK: Cambridge University Press, 1995.

———. *Language Play.* Chicago: University of Chicago Press, 1998.

———. *A Dictionary of Language,* 2nd ed. Chicago: University of Chicago Press, 1999.

———. *A Dictionary of the English Language: An Anthology.* New York: Penguin, 2005.

———. *txtng: the gr8 db8.* Oxford, UK: Oxford University Press, 2008.

Crystal, David, and Hilary Crystal. *Words on Words: Quotations About Language and Languages.* Chicago: University of Chicago Press, 2000.

Dalzell, Thomas. *Flappers 2 Rappers: American Youth Slang.* Springfield, MA: Merriam-Webster, 1996.

Davis, F. B. "Two New Measures of Reading Ability." *Journal of Educational Psychology* 33 (1942): 365–372.

Delahunty, Andrew. *Oxford Dictionary of Nicknames.* Oxford, UK: Oxford University Press, 2003.

de Ley, Gerd. *International Dictionary of Proverbs.* New York: Hippocrene Books, 1998.

Dickson, Paul. *Slang! Topic-by-Topic Dictionary of Contemporary American Lingoes.* New York: Pocket Books, 1990.

———. *Timelines.* New York: Addison-Wesley, 1990 (reprinted in 1991).

———. *What's in a Name? Reflections of an Irrepressible Name Collector.* Springfield, MA: Merriam-Webster, 1996.

———. *Labels for Locals: What to Call People from Abilene to Zimbabwe.* Springfield, MA: Merriam-Webster, 1997.

Douglas, Auriel. *Webster's New World Dictionary of Eponyms: Common Words from Proper Nouns.* New York: Simon & Schuster, 1990.

Editors of the *American Heritage®* Dictionaries. *Word Histories and Mysteries from Abracadabra to Zeus.* Boston: Houghton Mifflin, 2004.

———. *More Word Histories and Mysteries from Aardvark to Zombie.* Boston: Houghton Mifflin, 2006.

Editors of *Why Do We Say It? The Stories Behind the Words, Expressions and Clichés We Use.* Edison, NJ: Castle Books, 1985.

Ehrlich, Eugene. *What's in a Name? How Proper Names Became Everyday Words.* Darby, PA: Diane Publishing Company, 1999.

Elliott, Stuart. "With Banks Feeling the Heat, One in South Carolina Goes to the Kitchen." *New York Times,* November 12, 2008.

Espy, Willard R., and Orrin Hargraves. *Words to Rhyme With: A Rhyming Dictionary,* 3rd ed. New York: Checkmark Books, 2006.

Farb, Peter. *Word Play: What Happens When People Talk.* New York: Alfred A. Knopf, 1973.

Farkas, Anna, comp. *The Oxford Dictionary of Catchphrases.* Oxford, UK: Oxford University Press, 2002.

Flexner, Stuart Berg, and Anne H. Soukhanov. *Speaking Freely: A Guided Tour of American English from Plymouth Rock to Silicon Valley.* New York: Oxford University Press, 1997.

Forbis, Pat, and Sue Bartolucci. *Stedman's Medical Eponyms,* 2nd ed. Baltimore, MD: Lippincott Williams & Wilkins, 2005.

Freeman, Morton S. *The Story Behind the Word.* Philadelphia, PA: Institute for Scientific Information Press, 1985.

———. *A New Dictionary of Eponyms.* Oxford, UK: Oxford University Press, 1997.

Funk, Charles Earle. *A Hog on Ice & Other Curious Expressions.* New York: Harper & Row, 1948.

———. *Thereby Hangs a Tale: Stories of Curious Word Origins.* New York: Harper & Row, 1950.

———. *Heavens to Betsy! & Other Curious Sayings.* New York: Harper & Row, 1955 (reprinted in 1983).

Funk, Wilfred. *Word Origins: An Exploration and History of Words and Language.* New York: Wings Books, 1950.

G. & C. Merriam Company. *Webster's Elementary Dictionary: A Dictionary for Boys and Girls.* New York: American Book Company, 1945 (reprinted in 1949).

Gallant, Frank. *A Place Called Peculiar: Stories About Unusual American Place-Names.* Springfield, MA: Merriam-Webster, 1998.

Garrison, Webb. *Why You Say It.* Nashville, TN: Rutledge Hill Press, 1992.

Geller, Linda Gibson. *Wordplay and Language Learning for Children.* Urbana, IL: National Council of Teachers of English, 1985.

Glazier, Stephen. *Random House Word Menu.* New York: Random House, 1992.

Goldenberg, Claude. "Teaching English Language Learners: What the Research Does—and Does Not Say." *American Educator* 32, no. 2 (2008): 8–23, 42–43.

Golick, Margie. *Playing with Words.* Markham, ON: Pembroke Publishers, 1987.

Graves, Michael F. *The Vocabulary Book: Learning and Instruction.* New York: Teachers College Press, 2006.

Graves, Michael F. "Vocabulary Learning and Instruction." In *Review of Research in Education*, ed. Edward Rothkopf, 49–89. Washington, DC: American Educational Research Association, 1986.

Grossman, Deborah. "Word of Mouth: Menu Descriptors Are the Ultimate Cues for Flavor Expectation, So Choose Them Wisely," Summer 2008. http://www.flavor-online.com.

Grothe, Mardy. *Never Let a Fool Kiss You or a Kiss Fool You: Chiasmus and a World of Quotations That Say What They Mean and Mean What They Say.* New York: Viking, 1999.

Hall, Linda, ed. *Acronyms, Initialisms, and Abbreviations Dictionary*, 40th ed. Farmington Hills, MI: Gale Cengage, 2008.

Harris, Theodore L., and Richard E. Hodges, eds. *The Literacy Dictionary.* Newark, DE: International Reading Association, 1995.

Hart, Betty, and Timothy R. Risley. *Meaningful Differences in the Everyday Experience of Young American Children.* Baltimore: P. H. Brookes, 1995.

Haugen, Einar. "Short History of the English Language." In *The Barnhart Concise Dictionary of Etymology*, ed. Robert K. Barnhart, xvii–xxi. New York: Harper-Collins, 1995.

Hawkins, Del I., Roger J. Best, and Kenneth A. Coney. *Consumer Behavior: Building Marketing Strategy*, 9th ed. New York: McGraw-Hill, 2004.

Isil, Olivia A. *When a Loose Cannon Flogs a Dead Horse There's the Devil to Pay: Seafaring Words in Everyday Speech.* Camden, ME: International Marine, 1996.

Jeans, Peter D. *An Ocean of Words: A Dictionary of Nautical Words and Phrases.* Secaucus, NJ: Carol Publishing Group, 1993.

Johnson, Bonnie. *Wordworks: Exploring Language Play.* Golden, CO: Fulcrum Publishing, 1999.

Johnson, Bonnie von Hoff. *Wordworks: Exploring Language Play.* Golden, CO: Fulcrum Publishing, 1999.

Johnson, Dale D. *Vocabulary in the Elementary and Middle School.* Needham Heights, MA: Allyn & Bacon, 2001.

Johnson, Dale D., and Bonnie Johnson. *Ginn Vocabulary* Series. Lexington, MA: Ginn and Company, 1986.

———. *In So Many Words* Series. Logan, IA: Perfection Learning, 1990.

———. *The Brain Train* Game. Elizabethtown, PA: Continental Press, 1994.

Johnson, Dale D., Bonnie Johnson, Stephen J. Farenga, and Daniel Ness. *Stop High-Stakes Testing: An Appeal to America's Conscience.* Lanham, MD: Rowman & Littlefield, 2008.

Johnson, Dale D., Bonnie Johnson, and Kathleen Schlichting. "Logology: Word and Language Play." In *Vocabulary Instruction: Research to Practice*, ed. James F.

Baumann and Edward J. Kame´enui, 179–200. New York: The Guilford Press, 2004.

Johnson, Dale D., and Alden J. Moe. *The Ginn Word Book for Teachers.* Lexington, MA: Ginn and Company, 1983.

Johnson, Dale D., and P. David Pearson. *Teaching Reading Vocabulary.* Fort Worth, TX: Holt, Rinehart and Winston, 1978 (reprinted in 1984).

———. *Teaching Reading Vocabulary,* 2nd ed. Fort Worth, TX: Holt, Rinehart and Winston, 1984.

Kamil, Michael L., G. D. Borman, J. Dole, C. C. Kral, T. Salinger, and J. Torgesen. *Improving Adolescent Literacy: Effective Classroom and Intervention Practices: A Practice Guide* (NCEE #2008–4027). Washington, DC: National Center for Education Evaluation and Regional Assistance, Institute of Education Sciences, U.S. Department of Education. 2008. http://ies.ed.gov/ncee/wwc.

Kent, G. H., and A. J. Rosanoff. "A Study of Association." *American Journal of Insanity* 6 (1910): 37–96, 317–390.

Kintsch, Walter, and T. A. van Dijk. "Toward a Model of Text Comprehension and Production." *Psychological Review* 85 (1978): 363–394.

Kipfer, Barbara Ann, ed. *Roget's International Thesaurus: Revised and Updated,* 6th ed. New York: HarperCollins, 2001.

Knowles Elizabeth, ed. *The Oxford Dictionary of New Words.* Oxford, UK: Oxford University Press, 1997.

Lederer, Richard. *Get Thee to a Punnery.* Charleston, SC: Wyrick, 1988.

Lee, Laura. *The Name's Familiar.* Gretna, LA: Pelican Publishing Company, 1999.

Lepore, Jill. "A Nue Merrykin Dikshunary." In *Websterisms: A Collection of Words and Definitions Set Forth by the Founding Father of American English,* comp. Arthur Schulman, 1–35. New York: Free Press, 2008.

Levorato, Maria Chiara, and Christina Cacciari. "The Effects of Different Tasks on the Comprehension and Production of Idioms in Children." *Journal of Experimental Child Psychology* 60 (1995): 261–283.

Library of Congress. Great Depression and World War II, 1929–1945: President Franklin Delano Roosevelt and the New Deal, 1933–1945. Library of Congress, 2008. http://lcweb2.loc.gov/learn/features/timeline/depwwii/newdeal/newdeal.html.

Lighter, Jonathan Evan, ed. *Random House Historical Dictionary of American Slang,* vol. 1. New York: Random House, 1994.

———. *Random House Historical Dictionary of American Slang,* vol. 2. New York: Random House, 1997.

Lutz, William. *Doublespeak Defined.* New York: HarperCollins, 1999.

Manser, Martin H. *The Facts on File Dictionary of Proverbs*. New York: Checkmark Books, 2002.

McArthur, Tom. *The Concise Oxford Companion to the English Language*. Oxford, UK: Oxford University Press, 1996.

McQuain, Jeffrey. *Home-Grown English: How Americans Invented Themselves and Their Language*. New York: Random House, 1999.

Menand, Louis. "Thumbspeak: Is Texting Here to Stay?" *New Yorker*, October 20, 2008.

Mencken, H. L. *The American Language*. New York: Alfred A. Knopf, 1977.

Merriam-Webster OnLine. New Words, 2008. http://www.merriam-webster.com/info/new_words.htm.

Metcalf, Allan A. *The World in So Many Words*. Boston: Houghton Mifflin, 1999.

———. *How We Talk: American Regional English Today*. Boston: Houghton Mifflin, 2000.

———. *Predicting New Words: The Secrets of Their Success*. New York: Houghton Mifflin, 2002.

Mieder, Wolfgang. *The Prentice-Hall Encyclopedia of World Proverbs*. New York: MJF Books, 1986.

Mieder, Wolfgang, Stewart A. Kingsbury, and Kelsie B. Harder. *A Dictionary of American Proverbs*. New York: Oxford University Press, 1992.

Mieder, Wolfgang, and Barbara Mieder. "Tradition and Innovation: Proverbs in Advertising." In *Wisdom of Many: Essays on the Proverb*, ed. Wolfgang Mieder and Alan Dundes, 309–322. Madison: University of Wisconsin Press, 1994.

Miller, George A. *The Science of Words*. New York: Scientific American Library, 1991 (reprinted in 1996).

Moehringer, J. R. "Big Country." Review of *State by State: A Panoramic Portrait of America*, ed. Matt Weiland and Sean Wilsey. *New York Times Book Review*, October 12, 2008.

Morice, Dave. *The Dictionary of Word Play*. New York: Teachers & Writers Collaborative, 2001.

Morris, William, and Mary Morris. *Morris Dictionary of Word and Phrase Origins*, 2nd ed. New York: HarperCollins, 1977 (reprinted in 1988).

Nagy, William E., and Richard C. Anderson. "How Many Words Are There in Printed School English?" *Reading Research Quarterly* 19 (1984): 304–330.

National Institute of Child Health and Human Development. *Report of the National Reading Panel. Teaching Children to Read: An Evidence-Based Assessment of the Scientific Research Literature on Reading and Its Implications for Reading Instruction: Reports of the Subgroups* (NIH Publication No. 00–4769). Washington, DC: U.S. Government Printing Office, 2000.

Okrent, Arika. *In the Land of Invented Languages.* New York: Spiegel & Grau.

Onions, C. T., ed. *The Oxford Dictionary of English Etymology.* Oxford, UK: Oxford University Press, 1966.

Ortony, Anthony. "Understanding Figurative Language." In *Handbook of Reading Research,* ed. P. David Pearson, Rebecca Barr, Michael Kamil, and Peter Mosenthal, 453–470. New York: Longman, 1984.

Ostler, Rosemarie. *Dewdroppers, Waldos, and Slackers: A Decade-by-Decade Guide to the Vanishing Vocabulary of the Twentieth Century.* Oxford, UK: Oxford University Press, 2003.

Panati, Charles. *Panati's Extraordinary Origins of Everyday Things.* New York: Harper & Row, 1987.

———. *Words to Live By: The Origins of Conventional Wisdom and Commonsense Advice.* New York: Penguin Books, 1999.

Partin, Ronald L. *The Social Studies Teacher's Book of Lists.* Englewood Cliffs, NJ: Prentice-Hall, 1992.

Pearson, P. David, and Dale D. Johnson. *Teaching Reading Comprehension.* New York: Holt, Rinehart and Winston, 1978.

Pinker, Steven. *The Language Instinct: How the Mind Creates Language.* New York: William Morrow, 1994.

———. *Word and Rules: The Ingredients of Language.* New York: Perennial, 1999.

Random House. Words@Random. New Words: Sixty Years of New Words, 2008. http://www.randomhouse.com/words/newwords/.

RAND Reading Study Group. *Reading for Understanding: Toward an R&D Program in Reading Comprehension.* Santa Monica, CA: RAND Science and Technology Policy Institute, 2002.

Rawson, Hugh. "Slang: An Interview with J. E. Lighter." *American Heritage,* October 2003.

Rees, Nigel. *Dictionary of Catchphrases.* London, UK: Cassell Publishers, 1995.

Richler, Howard. *A Bawdy Language.* New York: Stoddart, 1999.

Ries, Al, and Laura Ries. *The Fall of Advertising and the Rise of PR.* New York: HarperCollins, 2002.

Roget, Peter M. *Thesaurus of English Words and Phrases, Classified and Arranged so as to Facilitate the Expression of Ideas and Assist in Literary Composition.* New York: Thomas Y. Crowell, 1852.

Room, Adrian. *NTC's Dictionary of Changes in Meanings.* Lincolnwood, IL: National Textbook Company, 1991.

Rosenberg, Scott A. "Judging Books by Their Covers: Graphic Designers Explain the Trade." *AM New York,* November 12, 2008.

"Scotland: Lost Forever." *New York Times*, February 28, 2004.

Shook, Michael D. *By Any Other Name*. New York: Prentice-Hall, 1994.

Short, Deborah J., and Shannon Fitzsimmons. *Double the Work: Challenges and Solutions to Acquiring Language and Academic Literacy for Adolescent English Language Learners—A Report to Carnegie Corporation of New York*. Washington, DC: Alliance for Excellent Education, 2007.

Snow, Catherine E., M. Susan Burns, and Peg Griffin, eds. Committee on the Prevention of Reading Difficulties in Young Children. *Preventing Reading Difficulties in Young Children*. Washington, DC: National Academy Press, 1998.

Soukanov, Anne H., and Kathy Rooney, eds. *Encarta World English Dictionary*. New York: St. Martin's Press, 1999.

Spears, Richard A. *NTC's Thematic Dictionary of American Idioms*. Chicago: NTC Publishing Group, 1997.

Sperling, Susan Kelz. *Poplollies & Bellibones: A Celebration of Lost Words*. Old Saybrook, CT: Konecky & Konecky, 1977.

Stahl, Steven A., and Katherine A. Stahl. "Word Wizards All!" In *Vocabulary Instruction: Research to Practice*, ed. James F. Baumann and Edward J. Kame´enui, 59–78. New York: Guilford Press, 2004.

Steinhauer, Jennifer, and Laura M. Holson. "Cellular Alert: As Texts Fly, Danger Lurks." *New York Times*, September 20, 2008.

Steinmetz, Sol, and Barbara Ann Kipfer. *The Life of Language*. New York: Random House Reference, 2006.

Strouf, Judie L. *The Literature Teacher's Book of Lists*. West Nyack, NY: Center for Applied Research in Education, 1993.

Thorndike, E. L., and Clarence L. Barnhart. *Thorndike Barnhart Beginning Dictionary*. Chicago: Scott, Foresman and Company, 1952.

Titelman, Gregory Y. *Popular Proverbs and Sayings*. New York: Gramercy Books, 1996.

———. *Random House Dictionary of Popular Proverbs and Sayings*. New York: Random House, 1996.

Urdang, Laurence, and Janet Braunstein. *Every Bite a Delight and Other Slogans*. Detroit, MI: Visible Ink, 1992.

Urdang, Laurence, Walter W. Hunsinger, and Nancy LaRoche. *A Fine Kettle of Fish and Other Figurative Phrases*. Detroit, MI: Visible Ink, 1991.

Wansink, Brian. *Mindless Eating*. New York: Bantam Dell, 2006 (reprinted in 2007).

Wen, Patricia. "E-Mail Address May Be Sending Wrong Message." *Boston Globe* Online, 2000. http://www.boston.com/dailyglobe2/ . . . may_be_sending_wrong _message+.shtml.

Westbrook, Alonzo. *Hip Hoptionary: The Dictionary of Hip Hop Terminology.* New York: Broadway Books, 2002.

Whipple, Guy, ed. *The Twenty-Fourth Yearbook of the National Society for the Study of Education: Report of the National Committee on Reading.* Bloomington, IL: Public School Publishing Company, 1925.

Zona, Guy A. *The Soul Would Have No Rainbow If the Eyes Had No Tears and Other Native American Proverbs.* New York: Touchstone, 1994.

Index

About the Authors

Dale D. Johnson is past president of the International Reading Association and professor of literacy education at Dowling College in New York. Prior to joining the Dowling faculty, he served as professor and dean of the College of Education and Human Development at the University of Louisiana and was a professor of education at the University of Wisconsin-Madison. Dr. Johnson has written numerous articles, chapters, instructional texts, and seventeen professional books including *Vocabulary in the Elementary and Middle School* and *High Stakes: Poverty, Testing, and Failure in American Schools.*

Bonnie Johnson is professor of human development and learning at Dowling College. She has written articles, chapters, six professional books including *Wordworks: Exploring Language Play* and *High Stakes: Poverty, Testing, and Failure in American Schools,* and more than fifty instructional texts for elementary, middle, secondary, and adult learners. Dr. Johnson has taught at all levels from preschool through graduate school and is the recipient of the University of Wisconsin's Distinguished Teacher of Teachers Award.